CHICAGO STUDIES IN THE HISTORY OF AMERICAN RELIGION

Editors

JERALD C. BRAUER
AND MARTIN E. MARTY

A CARLSON PUBLISHING SERIES

For a complete listing of the titles in this series,
please see the back of this book.

On Behalf of Israel

AMERICAN FUNDAMENTALIST ATTITUDES TOWARD JEWS, JUDAISM, AND ZIONISM, 1865-1945

Yaakov Ariel

PREFACE BY MARTIN E. MARTY

CARLSON
Publishing Inc

BROOKLYN, NEW YORK, 1991

Please see the end of this volume for a listing of all the titles in the Carlson Publishing Series *Chicago Studies in the History of American Religion*, edited by Jerald C. Brauer and Martin E. Marty, of which this is Volume 1.

Library of Congress Cataloging-in-Publication Data

Ariel, Yaakov S. (Yaakov Shalom), 1954-
    On behalf of Israel : American fundamentalist attitudes toward
Jews, Judaism, and Zionism, 1865-1945 / Yaakov Ariel ; preface by
Martin E. Marty.
        p.   cm. — (Chicago studies in the history of American
religion ; 1)
    Includes bibliographical references (p.) and index.
    ISBN 0-926019-39-2
    1. Dispensationalism—Relations—Judaism. 2. Judaism—Relations-
-Dispensationalism. 3. Fundamentalism—History. 4. Blackstone, W.
E. (William E.) b. 1841. 5. Gaebelein, Arno Clemens, 1861-1945.
6. Christian Zionism—United States—History. 7. Missions to Jews.
8. United States—Foreign relations—Israel. 9. Israel—Foreign
relations—United States. I. Title. II. Series.
BT157.A75 1991
261.2'6'0973—dc20   91-28112

Typographic design: Julian Waters

Typeface: Bitstream ITC Galliard

Case design: Alison Lew

Index prepared by Jonathan M. Butler.

Printed on acid-free, 250-year-life paper.

Manufactured in the United States of America.

Contents

An Introduction
to the Series

The *Chicago Studies in the History of American Religion* is a series of books that deal with topics ranging from the time of Jonathan Edwards to the 1970s. Three or four deal with colonial topics and three or four treat the very recent past. About half of them focus on the decades just before and after 1900. One deals with blacks; two concentrate on women. Revivalists, fundamentalists, theologians, life in the suburbs and life in heaven and hell, the Beecher family of old and a monk of new times, Catholics adapting to America and Protestants fighting one another—all these subjects assure that the series has scope. People of every kind of taste and curiosity about American religion will find some books to suit them. Does anything serve to characterize the series as a whole? What does the stamp of "Chicago studies" mean?

Yale historian Sydney Ahlstrom in *A Religious History of the American People*, as influential as any twentieth-century work in its field, pays respect to the "Chicago School" of American religious historians. William Warren Sweet, the pioneer in such studies (beginning in 1927) at Chicago and, in many ways, in America at large represented the culmination of "the Protestant synthesis" in this field. Ahlstrom went on to name two later generations of Chicagoans, including the seminal Sidney E. Mead and major figures like Robert T. Handy and Winthrop Hudson and ending with the two editors of this series. He saw them as often "openly rebellious" in respect to Sweet and his synthesis.

If, as Ahlstrom says, "a disproportionate number" of historians have some connection with the Chicago School, it must be said that the new generation represented in these twenty-one books carries on both the lineage of Sweet and something of the "openly rebellious" character that scholars at Chicago are encouraged to pursue. This means, for one thing, that the "Protestant synthesis" does not characterize their work. These historians question the canon of historical writing produced in the Protestant era even as many of them continue to pursue themes shaped in a Protestant culture. Few of them concentrate on the old "frontier thesis" that marked the early years of the school. The shift for most has been toward the urban and pluralist scene. They call into question, not in devastating rage but in steady patterns of inquiry, the received wisdom about who matters, and why, in American religion.

So it is that this series of books focuses on blacks, women, dispensationalists, suburbanites, members of "marginal" denominations, "ethnics" and immigrants as readily as it does on white men of progressive urban bent in mainstream denominations and of long standing in America. The authors relish religious diversity and enjoy discovering the power of people once considered weak, the centrality to the American plot of those once regarded as peripheral, and the potency of losers who were once disdained by winners. Thus this series enhances an understanding of an America overlooked by the people of Sweet's era two thirds of a century ago when it all, or most of it, began.

Rebellion for its own sake would not long hold interest; it might tell more about the psychology of rebels and revisers than about their subject matter. Revision, better than rebellion, characterizes the scholars. Re+vision: that's it. There was an original vision that characterized the Chicago School. This was the contention that in secular America and its universities religion mattered, as a theme in the national past and as a presence in the present. Second, it argued that the study of religious history belonged not only in the seminaries and archives of denominations, but also in the rough-and-tumble of the secular university, where no religious meanings were privileged and where each historian had to make a case for the value of his or her story.

Other assumptions from the earliest days pervade the books in this series. They are uncommonly alert to the environment in which expressions of faith occur. That is, they do not take for granted that religion comes protected in self-evidently important and hermetically sealed packages. Churches and denominations are porous, even when they would be sealed off; they cannot be understood apart from the ways the social environs effect them, but their power to effect change in the environment demands equal and truly unapologetic treatment. These writers do not shuffle and mumble and make excuses for their existence or for the choice of apparently arcane subject matter. They try to present their narrative in such ways that they compel attention.

A fourth characteristic that colors these works is a refusal in most cases to be typed in a fashionable slot labeled, variously, "intellectual" or "institutional" history, "cultural" or "social" history, or whatever. While those which concentrate on magisterial thinkers such as Jonathan Edwards are necessarily busy with and devoted to his intellectual achievement, most of the books deal with figures who cannot be understood only as exemplars in a sequence of studies of "the life of the mind." Instead, their biographies and circumstances come very much into play. On the other hand, none of these writers is a reductionist who sees religion as "nothing but" this or that—"nothing but" the working out of believers' Oedipal urges or expressing the economic and class interests of the subjects. Social history becomes in its way intellectual history, even if the intellects are focused on something other than the theologians in the traditions might like to see.

Some years ago *Look* magazine interviewed leaders in various denominations. One was asked if his fellow believers considered that theirs was the only true faith. Yes, he said, but they did not believe that they were the only ones who held it. The editors of this series of studies and the contributors to it do not believe that the "Chicago School," whenever and whatever it was, is the only true approach to American religious history. And, if they did, they would not hold that Chicagoans alone held it. To do so would imply a strange solipsistic or narcissistic impulse that would be the death of collegiality in the historical field. They have welcomed the chance to be in a climate where their inquiries are given such encouragement, where they find a company of fellow scholars in the Divinity School, the History Department, and the Committee on the History of Culture, whence these studies first emerged, and elsewhere in a university that provides a congenial home for massed and massive concentration of a special sort on American religious history.

While the undersigned have been consistently involved, most often together, in all twenty-one books, we want to single out a third person mentioned in so many acknowledgment sections, historian Arthur Mann. He has been a partner in two or three dozen religious history dissertation projects through the years and has been an influential and decisive contributor to the results. We stand in his debt.

Jerald C. Brauer
Martin E. Marty

Editor's Preface

An American can go through life without ever hearing or learning the word "dispensationalism." Most Americans do. Yet no American can understand foreign policy in respect to the Middle East, especially when Israel is the focus, without having to deal with a cohort of the population which is dispensationalist. That set of Americans is pro-Zionist and pro-Israel in steadfast, dogmatic, and inflexible ways. When an American president wanted to sell military planes to Saudi Arabia, dispensationalists bought full-page newspaper advertisements protesting the very thought of such sales. These planes could be used against Israel. Nothing America does should work against Israel's interest.

The reason people do not connect the word "dispensationalism" with such activity is that it lies buried in a larger project code-named "fundamentalism" or, sometimes, "evangelicalism." This book is the story of the rise of the dispensationalist wing of those movements and its attitude toward Zion. As Yaakov Ariel makes clear in this truly pioneering work, some English and American Protestants in the 19th century began to read the Biblical prophecies in a new way. They determined that the second coming of Jesus to begin a thousand year reign on earth demanded the restoration of Israel. America had to give political support to the founding of a nation of Israel to help make ready such a return, whose timing lay in God's hands.

Dispensationalists believed and believe that God deals with the earth in a set of successive "dispensations," in which humans are to respond in specific ways to show their obedience. Dispensationalists are, in their own way, "literalists." They believe that in the present dispensation they are to read biblical references to Israel literally, as referring not to a spiritual or figurative Israel but to a nation.

Yaakov Ariel came from Israel to do his research in the archives of Moody Bible Institute and other friendly fundamentalist centers. He there discovered and here offers in more detail and with more insight than had been shown before the ways the founders of the movement organized, propagated their views, and began to influence United States policy. Two characters stand out especially: William E. Blackstone, who twice took a "Memorial" to presidents, in 1891 and 1916, and Arno C. Gaebelein, who thought that pro-Israel sentiment also meant efforts to convert Israel.

As Ariel shows, there were thus Christian Zionists in America before Jewish Zionism came to prominence, and these Christians often resented the "secularism" of the Jews. The biggest surprise for those who have not read the writings of the four or five other historians who have worked with these resources, will be the discovery that fundamentalists, often believed to be anti-Semitic, came to be Israel's good friends. Ariel does not believe that Zionism and pro-Israeli sentiment meant that no forms of domestic anti-Semitism were present in the movement, but he will certainly contribute to the revision of the pictures most readers may carry about the line-up of "born again" Americans in respect to world political issues. One hopes that this work will fall into the hands of mass communicators and diplomats who have to interpret American foreign policy and the citizenry which contends over the directions it takes.

Martin E. Marty

Acknowledgments

This book began life as a doctoral dissertation written at the Divinity School of the University of Chicago. I am deeply grateful to Martin E. Marty for his guidance and encouragement. Working with him was a privilege. Arthur Mann and Jerald C. Brauer contributed observations and suggestions that enriched my work.

I have been fortunate in the assistance given me while researching and writing. Those who deserve special mention are: Walter Osborn of the Moody Bible Institute Library for helping me in my search for books; David Rausch assisted me in locating William Blackstone's personal papers; Wes Taber, manager of the American Messianic Fellowship in Chicago, allowed me access to Blackstone's papers as well as provided me with warm hospitality while I was studying them; David Green copyedited the entire draft and Roger Colson and Bonnie Honigsblum parts of it. Judith Hochberg not only typed the thesis with competence but showed interest and friendliness.

A number of foundations granted me scholarships that enabled me to pursue this inquiry: the Katherine J. Horwich Scholarship Fund; the Memorial Foundation for Jewish Culture; and the Woodrow Wilson National Fellowship Foundation, which provided me with a Charlotte W. Newcombe Doctoral Dissertation Fellowship.

The Hebrew University provided me with a postdoctoral fellowship that enabled me to pursue my work and revise the dissertation for publication. Of the few people who read this study and commented on it, I am especially indebted to Richard Polenberg of Cornell for his useful suggestions.

Special thanks go to members of my close family: to my parents, Batya and Aharon Ariel, for their support throughout the years of my study; to my wife, Rachel, who was instrumental in providing the conditions essential for scholarly work and shared the entire Chicago experience with me; and to our children, Yael, Nadav, and Tamar, who were a source of happiness throughout that period of our lives.

On Behalf of Israel

Background: Premillennialists and Their Attitudes Toward the Jews in American History

The Emergence of English Visionaries for Jewish Restoration

The Reformation that took place in England in the sixteenth century brought with it a new interest in the Jewish people who had been expelled from the realm in 1290. The translation of the Bible into the vernacular was to have a strong influence on the English Protestant mind, including its attitudes toward the Jews and the prospect of their return to Palestine.[1] The strong influence of the Bible in Elizabethan and Stuart England gave rise to new eschatological thinking. Previous Christian eschatology usually ignored the idea of a national Jewish restoration. At this time the return of the Jews to Palestine and their conversion to Christianity was to play a dominant role in prophetic interpretations and predictions.

One of the first to advocate the idea of a Jewish restoration to Palestine was the clergyman Francis Kett, who published his opinion in 1585. The Anglican church considered his book heretical, and Kett was executed by burning in 1589. Other visionaries of Jewish restoration and conversion followed.[2] One was Thomas Brightman, rector of Hawnes. Brightman predicted the defeat of the Turks, whom he identified with Gog and Magog, and the conversion of the Jews to Christianity and their restoration to Palestine. Jerusalem, he believed, would become the center of the universe and the newly established Christian church would serve as the center of Christianity.[3]

1

The lawyer Henry Finch published in 1621 *The Calling of the Jews*, which stirred much comment. He expressed his view that the Jewish nation would convert to believe in the Messiahship of Jesus and would be restored to Palestine. Finch insisted that the biblical references to Israel, Judah, Zion, and Jerusalem should be read literally and that the Old Testament prophecies that speak about the return of Israel to its land were therefore meant for the descendants of Abraham.[4]

Giles Fletcher, fellow of King's College, Cambridge, and ambassador of Queen Elizabeth to Russia, also expressed his belief in Israel's future restoration and conversion. Fletcher, who was considered an expert on Russian matters, believed the Tartars who dwelt near the Caspian Sea to be the ten lost tribes of Israel.

There were other visionaries of Jewish restoration and conversion in Elizabethan and Stuart England. Until the 1640s, however, they were individuals who acted on their own. One cannot talk yet about an English movement for Jewish restoration and conversion. These visionaries marked nevertheless the seeds and early beginnings of such a movement that was to appear later.

Premillennialism in Seventeenth-Century New England

The first generations of English settlers in what was to become the United States of America did not, by and large, hold to premillennialist convictions. Among the settlers of Virginia the hope for the Second Coming held no attraction at all. The situation was somewhat more varied among the Puritans in New England. However, there too premillennialism was not a prevailing creed.[5] The Puritans were concerned to build a perfect Christian polity in the new land. They considered themselves to have entered into a covenant with God, based on their perfect faith and saintly membership.[6] The New England Puritans often referred to their experience in the new environment in biblical terms, similar to those used to describe the sons of Israel.[7] Their eyes were thus not directed toward the literal Zion in Palestine. The settlers of New England possessed a great amount of hope for the building of the kingdom of God in America. The materialization of a perfect Christian polity through human effort seemed real. In such an atmosphere, the premillennialist hope for an imminent arrival of Jesus to build such a kingdom was not a common creed. Some Puritans did, however, express premillennialist convictions and included in their anticipation for the end of age both the conversion of the Jews and their restoration to Palestine.[8] These expressions of premillennialist interest in the Jews were to a large extent a continuation of similar manifestations in England of the sixteenth and early seventeenth centuries.

Increase Mather, a Congregationalist pastor in Boston and a leader of the Massachusetts Bay Colony, was the most noted New England Puritan to express the hope for the conversion and restoration of the Jews in relation to his hope for the imminent return of Jesus. Mather's concern was the Puritan hope of building the kingdom of God in America. The belief in the imminent Second Coming, in his eyes, made the need to keep the integrity and purity of a Christian society more urgent. Mather expressed the opinion that the conversion of the Jews to Christianity and their restoration to Zion would come as a prelude to the millennial age. The title of his major book, *The Mystery of Israel's Salvation*, which he published in 1669, bore witness to his concern with the future of the Jews.

An associate of Increase Mather who shared his hopes was the minister John Davenport. Like Mather, he was interested in building a perfect, saintly Christian polity and participated in the founding of New Haven, a stricter Puritan colony than Massachusetts. Davenport endorsed Mather's opinions in his preface to *The Mystery of Israel's Salvation*.[9] Davenport was impressed by Jewish expectations for national restoration that were stirred at that time by the appearance of the false Jewish Messiah Shabtai Zvi, rumors of which reached him in New England. He saw in that development a materialization of biblical prophecies.[10] Another supporter of the view of the Jewish future conversion to Christianity and return to Palestine was William Hooke, a colleague of Davenport at New Haven, who returned to England to serve as chaplain to Oliver Cromwell. He expressed his views on the matter in an additional preface to Mather's *Mystery of Israel's Salvation*.[11] Samuel Willard, a minister in Boston and acting president of Harvard College from 1701 to 1707, also expressed this belief in *The Fountain Opened: Or, the Admirable Blessings Plentifully to be Dispensed at the National Conversion of the Jews*.[12]

The premillennialist expectations concerning the Jewish people in seventeenth-century New England sometimes coincided with the efforts to convert the Indians.[13] Protagonists of the Christianization of the Indians argued that the Indians were the ten lost tribes of Israel. As the evangelization of the Israelites (Indians) had to precede the return of Jesus, priority should be given to missionary efforts among that people. In the late 1640s, for example, Edward Winslow, the agent of the Massachusetts Bay Colony in

London, lobbied in Parliament for financial aid for missionary work among the Indians on that basis. John Elliot, a missionary to the Indians, believed in the glorious future of the nation of Israel, in which he included the ten lost tribes, the Indians.[14] Cotton Mather, Increase's son and colleague, shared his father's premillennialist expectations. A missionary to Indians and blacks, he ardently desired the conversion of Jews. Unfortunately for him, there were no Jews around available for evangelization.[15]

The expectation that the Jews would convert to Christianity and be restored to Zion did not necessarily mean that their image improved in the eyes of the New England premillennialists. Their attitude could often be defined as a "theology of missions." As the Jews had not yet accepted Christianity, they were morally and spiritually deprived, and one might find many faults with them. After their conversion, however, they would change for the better. Their current wretched moral and spiritual condition was a good reason to work harder at their conversion.[16]

Although major figures among New England Puritans held the view of a future conversion and restoration of the Jewish people, no movement advocating these convictions came into being in seventeenth-century America. This was the hope of individuals. As prominent and influential in their community as they were, they represented in their ideas on the future of the Jews none but themselves.

Premillennialist Expectations and the Jews in Mid-Seventeenth-Century England

Whereas in New England premillennialist expectations regarding the Jews were the concern of few individuals, in England in the fifth and sixth decades of the seventeenth century these hopes stirred a movement that influenced the attitude of the English commonwealth toward the Jews. The civil war that began in England in 1642 gave rise in the Puritan camp to groups and individuals who anticipated the imminent return of Jesus. The new eschatological hopes often included the prospect of the Jewish conversion to Christianity and restoration to Zion as a precursor for the arrival of Jesus. The new premillennialist expectations had a direct effect on the actual attitude of the English commonwealth toward the Jews. Voices in the realm called for the cancellation of the Expulsion Act of 1290 and for the readmission of the Jews to England. Based on Deuteronomy 28:64, "The Lord shall scatter thee among one end of the earth even unto the other," they agreed that in order for the Messiah to come, the Jews had first to be scattered to all corners of the earth, including England. Another argument was that the readmission of the Jews to England would make them more available to efforts aimed at their evangelization and would therefore hasten their conversion to Christianity.[17] Some voices in the Puritan camp even suggested that England should take it upon herself to ship the Jews back to Palestine. In December 1655, Oliver Cromwell, the lord protector, summoned the Whitehall Conference to discuss the issue of the readmission of the Jews to England. He reiterated the aforementioned arguments in behalf of readmitting the Jews. Although the Whitehall Conference did not come out with a resolution that allowed free Jewish immigration to England, it did assert that there was no legal bar against it. In actuality, Cromwell allowed Jews to settle in the country. A year later, the Marranos that were living in London, disguised as Spanish and Portuguese, were allowed to express their Jewishness openly and to build a synagogue.

No similar movement appeared in New England at the time. The interest in the conversion of the Jews and their restoration to Palestine was much more intense in Britain and this situation remained unchanged until the last quarter of the nineteenth century.

The Rise of Postmillennialism

In the 1730s a new attitude toward the millennium gained ground in American Protestantism. Jonathan Edwards, the leader of the Great Awakening, advocated the idea that the millennium would be ushered in through human perfection. The arrival of Jesus to earth would take place after the millennium was fulfilled, not prior to it. The Jews, he believed, would convert to Christianity before the arrival of the Lord.[18] Edwards had the conviction that America had a role and a mission in spreading the true Gospel in the world. He, as well as other Protestants in America, did not abandon hopes for the building of the kingdom of God.

The hope of building a Christian America was to remain for a long time the hope of Protestants in that country.[19] In such an atmosphere, Edwards's view of the millennium as the period in which humanity prepares for the arrival of Jesus was to become normative for many Protestants in the eighteenth and nineteenth centuries. Americans had often viewed themselves as a redeemer nation, having a mission and role in building a better universe.[20] The Jewish nation did not occupy a particular role in this vision, and the reestablishment of a Davidic kingdom in Palestine was to remain for a long time the dream of insignificant groups and individuals in the American polity.

The Mormon Church and Jewish Restoration

A new religious leader who appeared on the American scene in the 1820s-1830s and showed interest in the future of the Jews out of eschatological conviction was Joseph Smith, the founder of the Church of Jesus Christ of Latter-day Saints. Smith, who grew up in Palmyra, New York, proclaimed himself in the 1820s to be a prophet of God. Moroni, a messenger of God, directed him, he claimed, to hidden golden plates, on which he found written the history of the members of the tribes of Joseph that had come to America after the destruction of the first temple. *The Book of Mormon*, which records Smith's revelations, thus tells the story of Lehi, who left Jerusalem with his family in 600 B.C.E. and was led by God to North America. With *The Book of Mormon*, Smith offered his followers a new sacred book to add to their canonical Christian scriptures. This addition to the Bible came to sanctify America as a God-given land for the sons of Joseph, whom the Mormons consider themselves to be.

Early Mormon history in America indeed resembled the biblical story of the sons of Israel who wandered in the wilderness until they reached the Promised Land. Settling first in 1830 in Kirtland, Ohio, the Mormons moved in 1837 to Independence and to Far West, Missouri. Driven by the hostility of their neighbors, they moved again to Nauvoo, Illinois. There, violence broke out again in 1844, and Joseph Smith was murdered. Under the leadership of Smith's successor, Brigham Young, the majority of the Mormons set out on a journey that brought them to Utah. Like the Puritans in seventeenth-century New England, the Latter-day Saints had built in the various steps of their journey and in Utah a polity that combined both the religious and the political dimensions. Mormonism was to remain more a community of believers than a regular denomination.

While Joseph Smith sanctified America as the promised land for the descendants of Joseph, he nonetheless held Palestine as the promised land for the descendants of Judah, the Jews, and foresaw both the restoration of the Jews to their ancient land and their conversion to Christianity:

And I will remember the covenant which I have made with my people; and I have covenanted with them that I would gather them together in my own due time, that I would give unto them again the land of their fathers for their inheritance, which is the land of Jerusalem, which is the promised land unto them forever, saith the father. And it shall come to pass that the time cometh, when the fulness of my gospel shall be preached unto them. And they shall believe in me that I am Jesus Christ, the son of God. . . . Then will the Father gather them together again, and give unto them Jerusalem for the land of their inheritance.[21]

The New Jerusalem in America thus did not come instead of the old Jerusalem in Palestine, but as an addition to it.[22]

In 1840, Joseph Smith sent a messenger to Palestine. Orson Hyde, an elder of the church, sailed to the Levant via England, where he tried to persuade English Jews to return to Palestine. In October 1841, the Mormon messenger prayed on the Mount of Olives to "let the land become abundantly fruitful when possessed by its rightful heirs."[23]

George J. Adams, who accompanied Hyde on his journey, remained in England to preach and spread the Mormon creed, declining to proceed to Palestine. In 1845, following the death of Joseph Smith, Adams left the Mormon church. Thereafter he led an adventurous life, changing homes, occupations, and wives. In early 1860, he settled in Indian River, Maine, where he organized a congregation that he named The Church of the Messiah. Adams claimed to have envisioned the end of times and asserted that the Holy Land would be saved and serve as a haven while the rest of the world would be destroyed. The Jewish nation, he asserted, would return to their land prior to the eschatological events. Influenced by his Mormon conviction, Adams considered Gentile believers to be the sons of Ephraim, while the Jews were the descendants of Judah. He pleaded with his congregants to settle in the Holy Land and serve as forerunners to the Jews and Gentiles who would follow them. They would witness, he promised, the arrival of the Messiah at firsthand. In 1866, with 155 followers, he settled in Palestine and established a colony near Jaffa. Obstacles were more numerous than the settlers had anticipated. One of the worst of them was the discovery of Adams's drunkenness. A year and a half after its establishment the colony disintegrated.[24]

After the death of Joseph Smith, Mormons showed only occasional interest in the fate of the Jewish nation.[25] On the whole they were too busy building the New Jerusalem in Utah to concern themselves with the old one and too involved in their own fate, which they considered to be that of Israel-Joseph, to pay much attention to Judah's. Far from seeking divine intervention, Mormons made and still make efforts to built a perfect, saintly society on earth.[26] Thus, although they believe in the eventual descent of Jesus to earth, their hope in that respect lacks the intensity and sense of imminence that characterizes the premillennialist conviction.[27] Unlike the dispensationalists in late-nineteenth-century and early-twentieth-century America, Mormons did not need to look at Zionism in order to gain self-assurance in their interpretation of prophecy. They have built a thriving polity, and in actuality eschatology played only a limited role in their religious system. Although *The Book of Mormon* foresaw a conversion of the Jews to Christianity, and although Mormons were engaged in aggressive missionary campaigns in which they recruited new members to their church, their attitude toward the Jews in the realm of evangelization was not different from their treatment of all other people. Mormons did not create any particular enterprises to Christianize Jews and did not lay special emphasis on evangelizing that nation.

The Church of Jesus Christ of Latter-day Saints dissented from the mainstream of American Christianity. The established churches looked on Smith and his disciples as heretics and lunatics. Isolated in their own territory, secluded from the bulk of American Christianity, the Mormon interest in the Jews, minimal and casual as it actually was, could not have had much effect on the attitude of the American polity in general toward the Jews and the prospect of their return to their land.

A Premillennialist Movement in the 1840s

The 1840s witnessed the first mass movement of premillennialist expectations in the United States. William Miller, a Baptist minister, roused a mass audience to expectation of the Second Coming when he predicted that Jesus would arrive in 1843. When nothing of particular significance happened that year, Miller shifted the arrival of the Lord to 1844—in vain, however. Miller's movement, which rebelled against the prevailing notion of the need to build the kingdom of God in America, was short-lived. When the expectants of the Second Coming realized that prophecy had failed, the movement disintegrated. Some of Miller's followers organized in the 1860s into the Seventh-Day Adventists, a dissenting denomination divorced from the center of American Christianity.

Miller had no place in his eschatology for the Jews. He followed the traditional Christian outlook that considered the Jewish role to have terminated with the appearance of Jesus. Nor did he consider Palestine to have any significance for the end of time. The Seventh Day Adventists followed Miller's attitude toward the Jewish people and the prospect of their restoration to Zion. Jesus, they believed, was coming in order to gather his true believers and take them to heaven, where the millennium was going to take place. Palestine therefore had no place in their eschatology.

Some followers of Miller thought otherwise. One of them was Clorinda S. Minor, who believed that Jesus would come to earth and that the Jewish people would return to Palestine. In 1852 she established a short-lived and ill-fated colony, Mount Hope, near Jaffa.[28] Small groups of Adventists who adopted similar convictions to those of Minor organized independently of the Seventh Day Adventists and continued to show interest in the Jews, their return to their land, and the prospect of their conversion to Christianity.[29]

Premillennialism and the Jews in Nineteenth-Century England

Whereas premillennialist movements in the United States in the first half of the nineteenth century divorced themselves from the center of religious life (and in the case of Miller's movement, had no role for the Jews) the situation was utterly different in England. There a revival of evangelicalism and premillennialist expectations occurred, and a very strong interest developed in the conversion of the Jewish people and their restoration to Palestine.[30] A series of eminent Englishmen, some of them associated with the established church, tried to promote in writings and deeds the conversion of Jews to Christianity and their return to their homeland. One of them was the seventh earl of Shaftesbury. In 1840, his persuasion brought the English foreign secretary, Lord Palmerston, to suggest that the Jews should be encouraged to settle in Palestine as an element that would be helpful in sustaining the Ottoman Empire.[31]

Most of the activity that resulted from the renewed English interest in the future of the Jews was concentrated in the field of missions. In 1808, the London Society for Promoting Christianity among the Jews was established.[32] It carried out the most ambitious evangelization efforts attempted among that nation, with about 200 missionaries who operated in more than 50 posts scattered in a few countries.[33] The society was active all through the

9

nineteenth century.[34] The establishment of other missionary societies aiming at converting Jews followed.

In the United States, in contrast, the missionary enterprises intended for evangelizing the Jews that were established up to the last quarter of the nineteenth century did not last long.[35] American Protestants at the time did not possess the same enthusiasm that their brethren in England manifested in that endeavor. Only with the rise of dispensationalism in the last quarter of the nineteenth century did the interest in the conversion of the Jews become as intense as it had been in Britain.

It was in this atmosphere of intensified eschatological expectations in Britain and of a new interest in the Jewish people and the prospect of their return to Palestine that dispensationalism, a new school of belief in the Second Coming of Jesus was born. The roots of American dispensationalism lie more in evangelical Britain of the first half of the previous century than in the United States.

TWO

Dispensationalism, a New Eschatological Belief, and the Jews

Premillennialism and Dispensationalism

Christian attitudes toward the idea of the millennium, the prospect of a kingdom of God on earth for a thousand years, fall into three categories: amillennialism, postmillennialism, and premillennialism. Amillennialists negate the idea of a literal materialization of a millennial kingdom and often interpret prophecies concerning this kingdom symbolically. This has been the prevailing attitude in Christendom since the fifth century C.E. Postmillennialism, a conviction that gained some ground among certain Protestant circles in the eighteenth and nineteenth centuries, is a belief that the millennial kingdom will materialize through human efforts. The spread of the Gospel and the implementation of Christian values will bring the world into perfection and then, after the millennium is established, Jesus will arrive.

Premillennialists, on the other hand, believe that Jesus will arrive to establish the millennium. According to their view, only divine intervention can bring salvation to humanity and turn the world into a righteous kingdom. Since the last quarter of the nineteenth century, the bulk of American premillennialists have been dispensationalists and dispensationalism has been the most influential eschatological school in this country.[1]

Eschatological Christian doctrines that divide human history into different dispensations (ages) are ancient and can be traced to sources as early as the Epistle of Barnabas, which was written probably at the end of the first century C.E.[2] Dispensationalist historians tend indeed to trace the roots of their movement to the early Christian writers, and try to show a continuum from ancient times through the Middle Ages and the Reformation to the present.[3] The modern eschatological belief known as dispensationalism has, however, distinct characteristics and cannot be regarded merely as the continuation of previous messianic convictions. The dispensationalist eschatology to which millions of Americans adhere today crystallized in Britain in the 1820s-1830s and is connected with the thought and deeds of John Nelson Darby and the group he led, the Plymouth Brethren.

John Nelson Darby and the Emergence of Dispensationalism

John Darby, who contributed more than anyone else to the shaping and spreading of dispensationalism, was born in London in 1800 to upper-middle-class parents of good education and social standing.[4] The family eventually moved to Ireland, where Darby studied law in Trinity College, Dublin. He then practiced law successfully for a few years until a conversion experience in 1825 caused him to abandon his profession and accept the position of curate in the Church of England (called the Church of Ireland, in Ireland). Darby ministered to a county parish (Wicklow) with great energy and enthusiasm. In 1827, he resigned his ecclesiastical post as a consequence of his disappointment with the established church.[5] He aimed at a more apostolic environment, similar to what he considered to be that of the early church. "The careful reading of Acts," he wrote many years later, "afforded me a practical picture of the early church, which made me feel deeply the contrast with its actual present state."[6]

Darby then developed a theory that was to serve as a cornerstone for dispensationalism. According to his view, "the Church of God, as He considers it, was composed only of those who were so united to Christ, whereas Christendom, as seen externally, was really the world and could not be considered as 'the Church.' "[7] For Darby, only true Christian believers (i.e., evangelical Protestants) comprised "the church," the body of the believers that would be saved and united with Christ. Consequently he advocated devotional offerings devoid of vestments, ornaments, choir, and musical instruments, as well as ordained clergy.

The ex-priest found in Dublin a few other persons who held similar views. They began to meet regularly for prayer, Bible study, and discussions. Similar groups emerged in a few more cities in Britain, among them London, Bristol, and Plymouth. In 1831 Benjamin W. Newton, the leader of the group in

Plymouth, invited Darby to come join the group. Darby gave the group its name, the Plymouth Brethren, which represented his understanding of the nature and aim of the group. It was not part of a regular, established church or denomination, but rather a spiritual fellowship of true believers in Christ.

Darby was a man of remarkable personality. Exceptionally energetic and highly charismatic, he exerted magnetic influence on people he encountered. His knowledge of French and German enabled him to embark on evangelistic campaigns not only in the English-speaking world but in foreign countries as well. The founder of the modern dispensationalist movement, however, could not tolerate opposition or criticism in his own camp. He preferred a small group that followed him over a large movement in which his ideas and position as a sole leader would be challenged. He reacted harshly to opponents, accused them of heresy, and brought about their isolation and expulsion from the Plymouth Brethren.[8] As a result, the Plymouth Brethren in Britain were preoccupied with endless internal quarrels, power struggles, heresy trials, and the like. Splits and factions occurred frequently, resulting in a growing number of opposing brethren groups that operated in Britain.

In addition, the membership of the brethren groups was elitist. Their members came from the aristocracy and the upper middle class. Among the members one could find judges, members of parliament, high-ranking officers in the army, and the like. The Plymouth Brethren was a dissenting group from the established church. With splits and quarrels in its ranks and with an inclination to be elitist and exclusive, the movement in Britain never became as widespread and influential as dispensationalism was to become in the United States.

The various brethren groups in Britain did not again unite until 1926. By then, premillennialism had a much smaller effect on the religious convictions and hopes of British society than it had had in the nineteenth century.

Dispensationalism—A New Eschatological Theory

Darby did not construct dispensationalism out of thin air. His contribution was, in large part, the shaping and crystallizing of earlier ideas concerning the Second Coming of Jesus. Darby's eschatological teaching, however, did differ in some major points from other premillennialist convictions. The prevailing premillennialist attitude prior to the rise of the Plymouth Brethren was historical or historicist.[9] That eschatological school claimed that the events at

13

the end of days had already begun and interpreted many historical events of the past as occurrences of the eschatological times.

Historicists have often engaged in determining the exact time at which the return of Jesus was supposed to take place. The Napoleonic Wars, at the end of the eighteenth century and the beginning of the nineteenth century, excited historicists and gave them hope that those events were the very last ones before the arrival of the Lord. Protestants have traditionally identified the pope as Antichrist. Premillennialists of the historicist school thus interpreted the exile of the pope from Rome by the French in 1798 as a fulfillment of prophecies in Daniel 7 and Revelation 13, which referred to the downfall of "the Beast" (alias Antichrist) after a reign of 1,260 days. Historicists have understood each day to mean a year.[10] They dated the rise of the papacy at 538 C.E. Thus, according to their calculations, the reign of the papacy lasted exactly 1,260 years and terminated in 1798.

Some historicists went one step farther. Concluding that Antichrist was crushed, they predicted the date of the arrival of Jesus. The most notable among them in America was William Miller. He based his calculations on Daniel 8:14, which, according to his view, predicted that 2,300 days after "the desolation of the sanctuary" the Messiah would come. Interpreting 2,300 days to mean years, he counted from the time of the destruction of the temple in Jerusalem by Nebuchadnezzar's army, an event he assumed to have happened in 457 B.C.E.[11]

Darby advocated a different type of premillennialism, known as futurism. Futurism, in contrast to historicism, expects the events of the end of times to occur in the future. Both schools expect the arrival of the Lord to occur in the near future. However, while historicists believe that most eschatological events happened in the past, futurists assert that the eschatological happenings have not yet begun. The latter often find signs that the present age (or dispensation) is terminating and that the eschatological events are to start very soon, but, according to their understanding, they have not yet started.

Futurism did not begin with Darby. Its first proponent was a Jesuit priest named Francisco Ribera, who, attempting to defend the papacy from Protestant accusations, suggested in 1590 that Antichrist could appear only after this age terminated.[12] It was Darby and the Plymouth Brethren, however, who turned futurism into a popular eschatological belief that competed successfully with the predominant historicist school. When Miller's prophecy failed to materialize, the historicist school of premillennialism received a severe blow, especially in America. Adventists, those of Miller's followers who continued to hold his hope, dissented from the mainline Protestant churches and created their own denomination, secluded from the center of American Christianity. The ground was clear for Darby to propagate his futurist ideas in the United States.

Darby introduced to futurist premillennialism a completely new theory that was to give dispensationalism one of its main characteristics, namely the idea of the secret, any-moment rapture of the church.[13] According to this belief, the descent of Jesus to earth would occur in two phases. In the first phase Jesus will not reach earth itself and will not yet begin his salvific mission. He will come to meet the church, the body of the true believers, in the air. This body of believers who might be raptured from earth at any moment would include both the living believers and the dead, who would rise from their graves and return to life. In the second and final descent, Jesus would come with his saints to earth, defeat Antichrist, and begin his reign on earth for a thousand years. In contrast to historicist interpreters of the end of time, dispensationalists usually refrained from predicting a particular time for the appearance of Jesus. They have asserted that it should occur soon, maybe right now; however, one does not know for sure.

Dispensationalists have occasionally differed as to where to place the rapture in the course of the eschatological events, whether it would occur prior to the Great Tribulation or in the middle of it.[14] Since the late nineteenth century, American premillennialists have almost unanimously held to the pre-tribulation rapture theory that originated with Darby. The rapture is thus expected, according to the prevailing theory, to be the starting point of the great events of the end of time.

Darby claimed that the rapture of the church correlated with its nature as a heavenly, spiritual entity;[15] dispensationalists have also seen the rapture as a vehicle to take the believers out of earth while the turmoil and horrors of the Great Tribulation were going on: "But the true Church which is not of the night (1 Thessalonians 5:5), being watchful and prayerful, will be accounted worthy to escape it, by the Rapture."[16]

The theory of the rapture of the church is one feature in their teachings that dispensationalists claim is based not merely on the Bible, but also on a private revelation.[17] Opponents of dispensationalism have indeed often accused Darby of brainpicking the idea of the secret rapture of the church.[18]

Another major attribute of dispensationalism that distinguishes it from previous eschatological teachings has been the place and role it ascribed to the Jewish people in the course of human history. Dispensationalists differentiate sharply between Israel and the church. In contrast to the traditional Christian understanding that identified the church as Israel, premillennialists recognize the Jewish people as the heirs of Old Testament Israel and the object of the biblical prophecies for the end of days.

In their view, God's covenants with Israel, the Jewish people, are still valid. These covenants include the Abrahamic covenant (Genesis 12:2-3), in which God promised to make Abraham the father of a great nation; the Mosaic covenant (Exodus 19-20), which was made between God and the whole nation of Israel, in which the Sons of Israel promised to keep the law; and the Davidic covenant (2 Samuel 7:4-17), in which God promised to keep David's royal house forever.[19] The sons of Israel in the Old Testament at times failed to honor their obligation under the Mosaic covenant. God, however, was still keeping his promises to Abraham and David. The prophets foresaw the rejuvenation of the covenants between God and his nation when the Messiah, who would be of David's descendants, would reign over a restored, glorified Israel, in its own land (e.g., Jeremiah 31:21-34, 33:15-16).[20]

Dispensationalists assert that God has assigned the church and Israel totally different roles in the course of history.[21] The church originally had no role. It came into being because the Jews refused to recognize Jesus as their Savior when he appeared for the first time and the kingdom could not materialize and was delayed. The current age, "the time of the Gentiles," is considered a parenthesis in the development of the ages. God, in some ways, had stopped the course of history and had introduced the church for the time being.

> The Messiah, instead of being received is cut off. . . . In place of ascending the throne of David, He goes to the cross. . . . God signified His sense of this act by suspending for a time His dispensational dealings with Israel. The course of time is interrupted. There is a great gap. Four hundred and eighty-three years are fulfilled; seven yet remain—a cancelled week, and all the time since the death of the Messiah has been an unnoticed interval—a break of parenthesis, during which Christ has been hidden in the heavens, and the Holy Ghost has been working on earth in forming the body of Christ, the church, the heavenly bride.[22]

The 490 years mentioned in this passage were based on the dispensationalist understanding of Daniel 9:24-27. Seventy weeks after a Gentile ruler issued a decree allowing the rebuilding of Jerusalem, the Messiah would come. In the first seven weeks of the seventy, the city would be rebuilt; sixty-two weeks later, the Messiah would appear but he would be rejected. In the last week, an evil ruler would be about to destroy the Jews, but the returning Messiah would stop him and restore the long-expected kingdom. Dispensationalists interpreted seventy weeks as 490 (seventy sevens) years. Thus, according to this view, 483 years had passed from the return of the Jews to Jerusalem, under Persian decree at the time of Nehemiah until the rejection and execution of Jesus. The last seven years of the Great Tribulation, in which Antichrist would appear, had not yet begun. Between the rejection of Jesus and the beginning of the seven years, there is this parenthesis, and history (the history of the Jews) has in some ways taken a break.[23]

In this dispensation the Jewish people do not serve any constructive function. They are scattered in the world and are often humiliated and harassed. Israel's role, however, has not terminated. In the next dispensation, the millennium, Israel will return to its position as God's first nation and will assume a leading role in kingdom, the very same role the Jews would have played had they accepted Jesus in his first coming. Thus, although dispensationalists have recognized the Jews to be God's chosen nation and have anticipated a great future for that nation, they have also expressed a certain amount of bitterness concerning the Jewish refusal to accept Jesus, which caused the delay in the advancement of the ages and the materialization of the kingdom.

Dispensationalists have not been the only ones in the history of Protestant eschatological hopes to have advocated the centrality of the nation of Israel for the Second Coming of Jesus. There have been premillennialists of the historicist school as well who have recognized the Jewish people to be God's chosen nation, which is destined to fulfill a decisive role in the eschatological times. Some British premillennialists of the historical school, for example, advocated the restoration of the Jews to Palestine in the seventeenth and nineteenth centuries. Historicists, however, varied on this issue. There never was a definite historicist view on the fate and role of the Jewish nation in God's redemptive plan. William Miller, the most noted premillennialist of the historicist school in nineteenth-century America, had no place for the Jews in his eschatological scheme. He followed the traditional Christian attitude toward the Jewish people.[24] In his view, they terminated their role as the nation of God with the arrival of Jesus and the establishment of the church. Modern dispensationalism is thus unique among Protestant premillennialists in its relation to the Jews. Dispensationalists have consistently and explicitly assigned the utmost importance to the Jewish people in their understanding of the course of human history and in their eschatological hopes.

17

Dispensationalism—A School of Biblical Hermeneutics

Dispensationalism is characterized not only by a distinct eschatological scheme, but also by a biblical hermeneutical system that has played a decisive role in shaping the attitude of dispensationalists toward the Jewish people and their return to their land. Dispensationalists consider the Bible to be the word of God, and as such divine and inerrant. Moreover, they believe that the Bible reveals God's plans for humanity, both for the present and for the future dispensations. According to that view, God did not leave humanity in the dark. The Bible provides clear guidance as to the prospect of human history. Premillennialists claim to have built their eschatological hopes and the details of their prediction of the events of the end of age on the biblical text. They substantiate the various stages and happenings of the messianic age with biblical passages. Premillennialists cut themselves off from Christian hermeneutical traditions that go back as far as the fathers of the church. Their only recognized authority is the Bible. They do pay tribute to Martin Luther (and the Reformation), but do not necessarily follow in his hermeneutical footsteps. While other hermeneutical traditions interpret biblical passages that speak about a perfected, peaceful future for the nation of God as having a symbolic meaning, premillennialists claim to read them literally. Emphasis on accepting the literal, obvious meaning of the Bible stands at the core of the dispensationalist apology. Other hermeneutical traditions, so dispensationalists claim, have been avoiding the simple, obvious, no-nonsense meaning of the biblical messages and have replaced them with sophisticated but misleading interpretations. They, on the other hand (so they believe) accept the original, truthful meaning of the Bible.

Premillennialists rejected the higher criticism of the Bible as an erroneous teaching, which, in their view, came to strip the Bible of its divine message and turn it into a profane book. Dispensationalists in America were among the founders of the fundamentalist camp that attacked views that denied the inerrancy of the Bible as well as fought other liberal trends such as the ecumenical movement and recognition of the legitimacy of other religious beliefs. If the Bible is divine and inerrant and is a source of guidance to humanity, there can be only one truthful school of obedience to God. To dispensationalists, only evangelical Protestants who have undergone a conversion experience and accepted Jesus Christ as their personal Savior walk in the light of God and they only shall be saved. All the others are walking in the dark, adhering to erroneous teachings or to none at all.

The dispensationalist hermeneutics of the Bible has been challenged by some biblical scholars as nonliteral. James Barr, for example, has asserted that fundamentalists in general tend to interpret biblical passages nonliterally in order to "save" the inerrancy of the Bible.[25] When a literal understanding of a biblical passage would mean that the story is nonsensical, the fundamentalists often choose an allegorical or symbolic interpretation.[26] As for the dispensationalist interpretation of prophetic passages, Barr claims that their aim is to fit the biblical text into the dispensationalist eschatological scheme, and the result is sometimes far from literal.[27] Dispensationalists, for example, interpret seventy weeks (of Daniel 9) as meaning 490 years.

Although premillennialist-dispensationalist hermeneutics of the Bible can be challenged as sometimes exceeding the simple literal meaning of certain biblical passages, it indeed can be evaluated as being on the whole more literal in its approach than other systems of biblical hermeneutics. There can be little doubt that the dispensationalist interpretation of "Israel" and "Jerusalem" is indeed literal. This literal understanding stands at the core of the dispensationalist attitude toward the Jewish people and Zionism. Premillennialists recognize the Jews as "Israel" and ascribe to them the biblical prophecies that speak about the future of that nation. Similarly, they recognize the earthly Jerusalem and the land of Israel as the actual scene where the messianic events would take place.

The dispensationalist distinction among the role of the church, the spiritual fellowship of true believers, and the earthly nation of Israel in the course of history is manifested in the method of the dispensationalist biblical exegesis. Certain prophetic passages in the Scriptures refer, according to that interpretation, to the Jewish people. Others are designated solely to the church. Other schools of biblical exegesis might point at times to some contradictions between prophecies in different books in the Bible. Premillennialists explain the differences by attributing them to different objects: some of them are intended for the Jews and some for the true believers in Christ.

Dispensationalism—A Philosophy of History

The name dispensationalism, by which this particular school of eschatology is known, stands for a philosophy of history. Dispensationalists believe that God has a different plan or economy for humanity in each dispensation or age.

Men are expected, according to their view, to respond in every dispensation to a different calling of God.[28] Most dispensationalists divide human history into seven such periods. Divisions of history differ slightly from one premillennialist thinker to another. Variations concern mostly the division of the first five ages. All dispensationalists agree that the last dispensation is the millennium and the current age is the one before the last. They are also in agreement that the current dispensation is nearing its end and the millennium is at hand.

Darby divided history into the following dispensations: paradisiacal state (to the flood); Noah (from the flood to the patriarchs); Abraham (until Moses); Israel (under law, under priesthood, under kings); Gentile; Spirit; and the millennium. Scofield divided human history into the following dispensations: innocency (in paradise); conscience (until the deluge); human government; promise (until Moses); law; grace; and kingdom.[29]

As a philosophy of history, dispensationalism is deterministic, for it asserts that history had a definite and predetermined course, which was decided by God and written in the Scriptures by his prophets. Ironically, the philosophy of history that gave dispensationalism its name is not unique to that teaching. There were other eschatological schools that also adhered to a view that divided history into different periods of time and assigned them different roles in God's plan for humanity. Dispensationalism is thus much more characterized as a unique school of eschatology by its biblical hermeneutics and by its eschatological scheme that differs in some major points from other visions of the end of age.

The Dispensationalist Eschatological Scheme and the Future of the Jews

According to dispensationalists the rapture of the church would mark the beginning of a period known as the Great Tribulation.[30] This period of time lies between the current dispensation and the millennium. In different terms, it begins with Jesus' coming for his saints and meeting them in the air and ends with Jesus' arrival on earth with his saints, to defeat Antichrist and begin his reign on earth. Most premillennialists expect that the Great Tribulation will last for seven years. Cyrus I. Scofield suggested three and a half years.[31]

As for the substance of this period, "There will be in it a period of unequalled trial, sorrow, and calamity (Daniel 12:1; Matthew 24:21), spiritual darkness and open wickedness (Luke 18:7; 2 Peter 3:2-4). It is the night of the world (John 9:41); Luke 17:34)."[32] For the Jews it would be "the time of Jacob's trouble."[33]

At the beginning of the Great Tribulation, 144,000 Jews (12,000 persons in each tribe) who have not yet accepted Jesus as their Savior would do so. They would recognize the events that would occur at that time as proceeding according to the Christian predictions they had heard from missionaries or read in pamphlets. These Jews would become apostles of the truth of the Christian message among their brethren and the nations.[34] They would be persecuted by Antichrist's government, and some of them would be martyred.

The Jews (or, according to some versions, part of the Jewish people) would return to their land prior to the rapture of the church, "in unbelief," without accepting Jesus as the Savior. They would establish there a state. But this state would by no means be the righteous glorious kingdom to which the biblical prophecies refer. The Jews would rebuild the temple in Jerusalem and reestablish the sacrificial service there. Antichrist would appear and would become the ruler of the Jewish state and the Jews would make a treaty with him.[35] Antichrist would be a Jew. In this aspect, dispensationalism breaks away from the traditional Protestant identification of the pope as Antichrist. Counterfeiting as much as possible, Antichrist would present himself as the true Messiah and as God. He would demand therefore to be worshiped as God and would enforce his rule by a reign of terror. Endless turmoil would characterize this period in the life of the Jews: famine, plagues, wars, and natural disasters such as earthquakes would cause death in unprecedented numbers. Only one-third of the Jewish people would survive these tormented years; the rest would perish.[36]

A series of wars would take place. Armies of four empires from all the corners of the earth—east, west, north, and south—would invade the country. Especially after the Bolshevik Revolution, dispensationalists have identified the northern power with Russia.[37] This power would be destroyed, as would other invaders.

The horror of the Great Tribulation would terminate in the Battle of Armageddon (Megiddo), a site in northern Israel. Jesus would come with his saints to destroy the forces of evil. He would defeat Antichrist and throw him alive into the lake of fire. Satan would then be bound and harmless for a thousand years. Jesus would judge the nations of the world. One of his criteria in carrying out judgment would be the behavior of nations throughout history toward the Jewish people, God's chosen nation. The millennium would begin. Jesus himself would be the king and ruler of the world. He would install peace and justice. The capital of the world would be Jerusalem, where the restored nation of Israel would fulfill the administrative functions of the new kingdom.

The remnant of the Jews who would survive the Great Tribulation would recognize Jesus as their Lord and Savior. Moreover, they would turn into an evangelizing nation and become instrumental in spreading the true belief in God among the nations of the earth. The temple would be rebuilt and sacrificial service would be carried on there. There is, however, no basis to the claim that the millennium would therefore have a Jewish character.[38] In the dispensationalist view of the millennium, postbiblical rabbinical Judaism would cease to exist. Much of the religious and cultural heritage of the Jews that derived from the oral law, for example, would be abandoned. The Jews would become honorable citizens of the new kingdom, they would be the Brahmins of the millennial commonwealth. But it is a mistake to suggest that their religion and civilization would prevail in the new order.

The religious and peaceful reign of Jesus on earth would last for a thousand years. At the end of this time the world would again go through a metamorphosis. Satan would be released and would rebel for the very last time. Jesus would crush Satan and his followers, who would be defeated forever, never to rise again. Cosmic changes would then take place. There would be "a new heaven and a new earth." Jesus would present his kingdom to God, the father. The dead would be resurrected and God would pass judgment upon them. The eternal kingdom of God would thus be ushered in, to last for evermore.

Analysis of the place and role of the Jewish people in the dispensationalist eschatological scheme reveals unmistakably the centrality of Israel in these messianic hopes. It is evident that the Jewish people are essential for many of the events of the end of age to get going. Premillennialists have therefore taken a close interest in the fate of the Jews and in the developments that have occurred to that nation. They have interpreted these events in light of their eschatological convictions. As the dispensationalist eschatological scheme predicts the partial return of the Jews to their land "in unbelief" prior to the arrival of Jesus, the premillennialists saw in the Zionist immigration to Palestine a fulfillment of biblical prophecies. In certain instances they worked to promote and advance Jewish resettlement in the Promised Land. Similarly, premillennialists have seen it as their duty to spread the knowledge of Jesus' messiahship among the Jews. One reason for that was the need that at any given moment, 144,000 Jews should possess that knowledge, so that they could recognize the truth of the Christian message, once they witnessed the first dramatic events of the end of time, and convert.

THREE

The Spread of Dispensationalism in America

The 1860s to the 1920s were the formative years for the shaping of dispensationalism in the United States. During this period, the new eschatological conviction became a united and stable movement that influenced millions of Americans. Evangelists, publications, prophetic conferences, and teaching institutions were instrumental in spreading the new messianic hope in America. They made the dispensationalist outlook on the Jewish people and its role in the events of the end of age part of the creed of many evangelical Protestants in this country.

Dispensationalism started to spread in the United States in the 1860s. John N. Darby, the man who shaped the new conviction, visited America to disseminate his ideas. From 1862 to 1878, he made seven trips to the United States and Canada, lecturing, meeting ministers, and teaching the Bible in small groups. Though Darby established groups of brethren in the country, his main achievement was in the impact of his dispensationalist teaching on members of mainline Protestant denominations.

In its early years in America, dispensationalism attracted a few Episcopalians and occasionally a few Lutherans, but this became more and more an exception to the rule. Dispensationalism found its adherents mostly among denominations whose roots went back to the reform tradition as well as to nineteenth-century revivalism in America: Presbyterians, Baptists, Methodists, and Congregationalists. In Britain Darby's followers often dissented from the established churches, but in America converts to dispensationalism usually remained active members of their churches. As a consequence, in America dispensationalism was characterized as a legitimate belief held by respectable and even prominent members of major Protestant churches. Moreover, in America dispensationalism avoided much of the schism and factionalism that characterized the movement in Britain, one reason being that in the United States the new eschatological school did not associate itself with a single, charismatic leader.

In its first decades, dispensationalism did not become a mass movement of the kind Miller had succeeded in gathering with his predictions of the end of days, prior to the disappointment of 1844, when prophecy failed. The progress of dispensationalism was slower, but it eventually gathered strength and became a conviction accepted by millions and a stable movement whose impact on American religious life has lasted over a hundred years.

James H. Brookes and the Niagara Conferences

One of the most noted early converts to and activists of dispensationalism in America was James H. Brookes, a Presbyterian minister from St. Louis, Missouri. Brookes published a series of books that popularized the belief in the imminent Second Coming of Jesus. The books were bought by thousands of evangelical Protestants in the English-speaking world. The most widely circulated was *Maranatha: or the Lord Cometh* (1874). In *Maranatha*, Brookes spent 545 pages elaborating the dispensationalist belief, its scriptural hermeneutics, and its eschatological scheme and understanding of God's plan and purpose in the ages. He devoted a long chapter to describing what he considered to be the role of the Jews in the end of days. Brookes found it necessary to convince readers of the continuing validity of God's promise to the Jewish people and of the glorified future that awaits that nation.[1] He made numerous references to the Scriptures, insisting that his readers read those passages literally.

Brookes wrote another popular, much shorter book on the Second Coming of Jesus: *I am Coming*.[2] It included a chapter dedicated to the dispensationalist understanding of the history and future of the Jewish people in relation to the events that would precede and follow Jesus' return to earth.

From Moses to Malachi, and from Matthew to Revelation, there is abundant and unvarying testimony that the literal descendants of the literal Abraham and Isaac, and Jacob, shall be literally scattered among all nations, as a punishment for their sins, and in the last days, shall be literally restored to their own land,

and rejoice once more in the covenant relations to Jehovah, as the head of the millennial nations.[3]

Brookes was impressed by the Zionist immigration to Palestine that began in the 1880s, seeing in it a vehicle for fulfilling God's plans. "Even now the covenant-keeping God is preparing the way for the return of their posterity to the land of their fathers."[4]

In 1875, Brookes started publishing a dispensationalist periodical, *The Truth*. Until the end of his life, he both edited the paper and wrote a large part of its content, including a few articles that expressed his opinion concerning the fate of the Jewish people.[5] As he had in *Maranatha*, Brookes again felt the need to make a special effort to persuade his readers of the dispensationalist view that the Jewish people were God's chosen nation, which had been assigned a glorified role in the millennial kingdom. Brookes evidently assumed that some readers might have difficulty accepting this new outlook. He knew how strongly rooted was the traditional Christian position that denied the Jews their role as the heirs to the covenant between God and Abraham and transformed it to the church. As with other protagonists of dispensationalism, Brookes, in his efforts in this direction, leaned on a literal reading of the biblical promises to Israel.

> Along with the promise of Christ's second advent comes the clear explicit, unconditional and oft-repeated promise of Israel's return to their own land, of their conversion, and of their dignity and glory during the millennial age. It is difficult to understand how any unprejudiced reader of the Bible, can read such distinct testimonies as the following, and then retain the slightest doubt concerning the future restoration, enlargement, and blessedness of the now despised and scattered Jews.[6]

The editor of *The Truth* sought to combat the antagonism to Jews that he felt was common among Christians. Like many dispensationalists, Brookes saw himself as an enemy of anti-Semitism.

> Thus if we remember that God's revelation came to the Jews, and that through them the same great revelation came to us, it will be easy to see that salvation is of the Jews. Surely this fact should be sufficient to rebuke the contempt and hatred which is so commonly manifested toward them by professing Gentile Christians, who do not remember what they owe to the people they despise. Rather should they remember the divine command. "Pray for the Peace of Jerusalem: they shall prosper that love thee," Ps cxxii:6.[7]

27

Brookes took special interest in the evangelization of Jews. He himself was not engaged in missionary work among that nation, but nevertheless he tried to promote his ideas concerning that realm. Brookes's opinion represented a drastically new approach on the part of dispensationalists in their attempts to Christianize Jews. He asserted that Jews who accepted Jesus as their Lord and Savior should not be asked to gentilize and turn their backs on the Jewish community to which they belonged. They had no need to join Gentile churches.[8] Dispensationalists, he believed, were better suited to preach the Gospel to the Jews than were nonpremillennialists. Their Christian message included a prospect of hope and glory for the Jewish people, a prospect that correlated with the Jewish hopes of restoration to Zion. Their dispensationalist message was therefore more likely to be accepted.

> It is of no use to ask these people to join gentile churches. . . . No man is fit to preach to the Jews unless he believes in the personal coming of the Messiah. He must go to them with the message, "Behold, the days come, saith the Lord, that I will raise unto David a righteous Branch, and a king shall reign and prosper. . . . In His days Judah shall be saved, and Israel shall dwell safely." . . . All Jews, except those who have become utter infidels, confidently expect to be restored to the land of their fathers and it is most important to show them that their hope is founded upon Jehovah's immutable covenant, and that it shall be fulfilled by the coming of the Messiah.[9]

Brookes praised dispensationalist missions to the Jews that he thought were implementing the principles he was advocating. He marveled at Joseph Rabinowitz's Christian Synagogue in Kishineff, Russia, and looked favorably at Arno C. Gaebelein and Ernest Stroeter's attempt to establish a congregation of Christian Jews in the Lower East Side of New York.[10]

Brookes, who opposed the hostile attitude of Christians toward Jews and who called for an appreciative and amicable approach toward those he considered to be God's chosen people, was himself not completely devoid of prejudices against that nation. Brookes's understanding of the behavior of Israel in the time of the Bible was expressed in unfavorable traditional Christian terms.[11] Perhaps the most striking example of Brookes's ambivalent attitude toward the Jews is contained in the following passage, in which he both defends the Jews and affirms disturbing prejudices against them:

> Nine-tenths of the Americans say that the Jews are a mean race, and if they are meaner than the Gentiles, considering the blessings and the privileges the latter have received, they must be mean indeed. It is probable that if our ancestors had

been banished and expelled, kicked and cuffed, robbed and murdered for centuries the world over, we too would feel like raising our hand against every man. The Gentiles in view of the past, and what they ought to know of themselves at present, should be slow to speak of the meanness of the Jews.[12]

James H. Brookes was the living spirit and leader of a series of Bible-study conferences known as the Niagara Conferences. Conferences devoted to study of the Bible and prophecy were one of the major vehicles of the dispensationalist movement in America in the last quarter of the nineteenth century.[13] The conferences provided American premillennialists with forums in which to express their beliefs and propagate them as well as with a meeting place in which to exchange ideas. The Bible and prophecy conferences helped American dispensationalism turn into a more coherent and united movement. It was through these conferences, for example, that the pretribulation rapture gained prominence in American dispensationalism, suppressing the other options concerning the rapture theory, namely the midtribulation rapture and posttribulation rapture.

The Niagara Conferences' official name in their early years was The Believers' Meeting for Bible Study.[14] The first was a small informal conference held in New York City in 1868. In 1875, a conference was summoned in Chicago, thereafter to meet annually in the summer for one or two weeks. From 1883 to 1897, the conference met at Niagara, Ontario (whence it derived its name).

In 1878, Brookes drew up fourteen articles or "Fundamentals of Faith," which were to serve as the common ground upon which all of the participants of the Bible-study conferences agree. In 1890, it was officially adopted by the Niagara Conference as its creed. The document manifests the premillenialist movement's close ties with the conservative, fundamentalist impulse in American Protestantism, which was developing as an important movement in those years as well.

The "Fundamentals of the Faith" were published in a pamphlet that was distributed long after the Niagara Conferences had ceased to convene. Regarded by premillennialists as a statement of faith in general, the document started with a declaration of purpose, namely to combat the secular and liberal trends in Christendom. According to statements in the creed the Bible was divinely inspired and revealed God's instructions to humanity. Another article asserted that "no one can enter the kingdom of God unless born again." A further statement promised that "all who are born again . . . through faith in

Christ are assured . . . of their salvation." The last article refers to the eschatological events.

> We believe that the world will not be converted during the present dispensation, but is first ripening for judgment, while there will be a fearful apostasy in the professing Christian body; and hence that the Lord Jesus will come in person to introduce the millennial age, when Israel shall be restored to their land.[15]

In "The Fundamentals of the Faith," the return of the Jews to their land, being part of the dispensationalist eschatological hope, was thus linked to a broader creed, that of the emerging fundamentalist movement. It was in this segment of American Protestantism that the dispensationalist hope found a home, and it is in it that the belief in the role of restored Israel in the eschatological events and time received growing acceptance.

Dwight L. Moody and His Attitude Toward the Jewish People

The dispensationalist movement associated itself directly with the revivalist tradition when Dwight L. Moody, the leading evangelist in America during the last quarter of the nineteenth century, became a dispensationalist.[16]

Born in Northfield, Massachusetts, in 1837, Moody settled in Chicago in 1855, where he became a successful merchant. In Chicago he underwent a conversion experience, after which he devoted part of his time to working as a Sunday school instructor. Moody later decided to give up his business altogether, in order to dedicate himself completely to evangelism. Moody's career as a revivalist developed throughout the 1860s. In 1873, he visited Britain, conducting a revivalist campaign there together with the gospel singer Ira Sankey. After his return from England, Moody became the leading revivalist in America. His revival meetings were often conducted in the major cities and were larger than any previously held in America. The administration of Moody's revival campaign demanded organizational skills similar to those required to run a large business enterprise.

Revivals were intended in the spiritual sphere to bring the lost sheep to their Savior, Jesus. On a more practical level, they were meant to bring the unchurched to the church (more accurately, the Protestant churches). The sermons preached in the revival meetings were intended to make individuals in the audience recognize their sinfulness, their hopeless spiritual condition, and the eternal damnation that awaited them. The sermons further emphasized the urgent need to repent and seek salvation through the acceptance of Jesus as Lord and Savior. Many who attended revival meetings would indeed undergo a deep emotional and spiritual metamorphosis (often called "regeneration"). They would join the church and henceforth were to lead holy lives. Moody's message was intended to bring his audience not only to accept Jesus and join the church, but also to lead a life based on middle-class morality. To be a true Christian believer meant, as a matter of course, to be an active and productive member of the community.

Moody had first been exposed to dispensational teachings in the late 1860s. During the 1870s he met John Nelson Darby, the leader of the Plymouth Brethren, several times. Moody's acceptance of the belief in the imminent return of Jesus added strength and prestige to the movement. In addition, he became a patron of dispensationalism. Moody invited dispensationalists to the biblical conferences he organized in Northfield, Massachusetts, thus offering the theoreticians of the movement a forum and a place to meet. He was instrumental in establishing the Bible House in Chicago, which became a major center for training activists of the premillennialist movement.

Moody, on the whole, was a believer in the premillennialist hope of the second coming of Jesus.[17] He incorporated dispensationalism into his understanding of his role and mission as an evangelist. In one of his sermons, Moody asserted: "I look on this world as a wrecked vessel. God has given me a life-boat and said to me: 'Moody, save all you can.' "[18] Yet he only partially incorporated this conviction into his evangelistic message and did not use the eschatological theme very often in his sermons.[19] One cannot therefore accept James Findlay's suggestion that Moody found dispensationalism a convenient and useful tool for bringing his audience to conversion.[20] Dispensationalism, according to Findlay, gave a notion of urgency to the need to be converted. While Moody did not very often use the dispensationalist eschatological theme in his sermons, evangelists following him did, and the eschatological dispensationalist message has been an essential part of mass evangelism in America in the twentieth century.[21]

Although Moody did not devote full sermons to his ideas on the Jewish people, he referred extensively to them in his preaching. His thoughts concerning that nation represented many common prejudices against Jews, as well as the influence of dispensationalism on his thought. In Moody's view the Jews were the sinning sons of Israel who disobeyed God.[22] They were the people who failed to help their neighbor in the famous parable of the Good

31

Samaritan.[23] They were the vicious crowd that preferred the execution of Jesus to that of Bar-Aba,[24] humiliated Jesus on his last journey, along the Via Dolorosa,[25] and cried out "let his blood be upon us and upon our children."[26] The destruction of Jerusalem and the temple, in 70 C.E., came as a prophesied punishment for the wickedness of the Jews.[27]

The Jews' worst sin was their unwillingness to recognize Jesus as their Lord and Savior.[28] It was this stubborn act that earned the Jews their position as outcasts: "The Jews were cut off on account of their unbelief. We were grafted in on account of our belief."[29] Moody believed in the stereotype of the Jews as greedy and materialistic. Preaching on the Good Samaritan, he said: "You know a Jew must have a very poor opinion of a man if he will not do business with him when there is a prospect of making something out of him."[30] When Moody was in need of an example of a rich man he used Rothschild.[31]

As prejudiced against Jews as he might have been, Moody was not an anti-Semite. His attitude toward the Jewish people included elements of appreciation and hope. Moreover, although Moody's stereotypical view of Jews was on the whole not a positive one, it was far from demonic or diabolic. He never launched an attack against the Jews or blamed them for any of America's troubles or faults. He did not use the Jews as a scapegoat. Furthermore, Moody never suggested that the Jews should be punished for their bad deeds or ugly characters, or that any kind of restrictions should be imposed on them, such as stopping Jewish immigration to America, for example.

Moody was not original in his criticism of the Jews. He followed a long and well-paved route of Christian outlooks on the matter. Moody's prejudices probably reflect views that were common in many segments of Protestant America at the time.

Moody developed his image of the Jews from his reading of the Scriptures. He had very little knowledge of postbiblical Judaism. In one passage he says, "Diana, Apollo, the Pharisee and Sadducee are no more, but the despised Christians yet live."[32] Moody was ignorant of the fact that orthodox Judaism (and in a way also nonorthodox Judaism) sees itself as a continuation of the Pharisaic tradition.[33] Moody probably had very few personal encounters with Jews. The 1880s and 1890s witnessed vast Jewish immigration to America from the small towns of Eastern Europe. Most of these Jews came to America penniless and inhabited the poor areas of the urban centers. They were no Rothschilds.

In the winter of 1875-76 an incident occured concerning Moody's remarks on Jews. The evangelist was quoted saying that in 1873 Jews in a meeting in

Paris boasted over the killing of Jesus.[34] Jewish leaders in the United States protested angrily.[35] Moody later claimed that he was misquoted and added that he respected Jews.[36]

Public criticism approached Moody again in 1893 when he invited Adolf Stoecker, the notorious German anti-Semitic preacher, to carry out evangelistic work with him in Chicago.[37] Moody rejected the newspapers' accusations against Stoecker: "We give you a warm welcome. God bless you. We don't believe the newspapers. We believe the Bible. We have confidence in you. We love you."[38] Moody might have believed in good faith that Stoecker was innocent and that the accusations against him were part of a campaign to undermine the German preacher's work.[39] The American revivalist looked on Stoecker as a fellow evangelist who was undertaking in Germany the same kind of work he was doing in America, and therefore he trusted him. He did not bother to check the accusations against Stoecker. Jews viewed the matter differently. For them, Moody's welcome to Stoecker meant an endorsement of his views. They developed a suspicious and contemptuous attitude toward Moody. Among other things, Jews associated Moody with missionary enterprises attempting at their conversion. For them such attempts were insults to their religious heritage as well as a threat to Jewish survival.[40] An illustration of the suspicion that Jews developed toward Moody could be found in Isaac Mayer Wise's reaction to the evangelist. Alarmed by Moody's remarks on the Jewish involvement in Jesus' humiliation and crucifixion, this outstanding leader of reform Judaism asked Moody to debate the deicide charge with him, but to no avail.[41]

The eschatological treatment of the Jews is the one feature of dispensationalist thinking that clearly influenced Moody. Although he was prejudiced against Jews, Moody had great hopes for their conversion and restoration to Palestine, and to their old position as the nation of God. On a few occasions Moody predicted Israel's future:

> When Christ returns, He will not be treated as He was before. There will be room for Him at Bethlehem. He will be welcomed in Jerusalem. He will reveal Himself as Joseph revealed himself to his brethren. He will say to the Jews "I am Jesus," and they will reply: "Blessed is He that cometh in the name of the Lord" and the Jews will then be that nation that shall be born in a day.[42]

This passage expresses an understanding of the place of the Jews in God's plan for humanity that is identical to that of nineteenth-century dispensationalists. The biblical prophecies for the end of time are meant for the Jews. It is

33

interesting to note that the scene, the place where Jesus is going to meet his brethren, is in the Holy Land. It was a common dispensationalist assumption that the Jews would already be restored to their land by then.

In another instance, while discussing God's promise to Abraham (Genesis 22:17-18), Moody expressed his appreciation for the long endurance of the Jewish nation as well as what he considered the outstanding achievements of the seed of Abraham.

> Hasn't that prophecy been fulfilled? Hasn't God made that a great and mighty nation? Where is there any nation that has ever produced such men as have come from the seed of Abraham? There is no nation that has or can produce such men. . . . That promise was made 4000 years ago, and even now you can see that the Jews are a separate and distinct nation. . . . You can bring almost every nation here and in fifty years they will become extinct, merged into another; but bring a Jew here and in fifty years, a hundred years, or a thousand years, he is still a Jew. When I meet a Jew I can't help having a profound respect for them, for they are God's people.[43]

In another place Moody said:

> I challenge any infidel to put his finger on any promise which God has not kept. For 6,000 years the devil has been trying to find that God has broken His word. What a jubilee there would be in hell to-day if they found God had broken his word! Didn't He keep his word with Adam, and Abraham, and Moses? Isn't every Jew a monument of God's word?

Moody spoke further on the future of the Jewish people: "I have an idea that they are a nation that are to be born in a day, and when they are converted and brought back to Christ, what a mighty power they will be in the land, what missionaries to carry the glad tidings around the world."[44]

Jesus himself, he reminded his audience, was a Jew.[45] He claimed that Jesus, when he was on the cross, had sent his disciples back to Jerusalem "to preach the Gospel to the men who had crucified him."[46] The very same idea is expressed in another place: it was Christ's "command" that his message be preached first and foremost "to those Jerusalem sinners."[47]

Moody saw no contradiction between his sometimes unpleasant opinions of Jews and his hopes for their conversion, their return to Palestine, and their rebirth as God's nation. In his view, though the Jews may have treated Jesus viciously and rejected him, Jesus himself did not abandon hope for them, and he himself ordered his disciples to preach the Gospel to them. They are still

Jesus' brethren. As wicked as they might have been in the past and as greedy as they may be in the present, in the future they will assume a new role, when they accept Jesus. The Jews were punished for their stubbornness but will be restored to their glory when they recognize their savior. God will firmly keep his promises to them.

The Northfield Conferences

The Bible conferences Dwight L. Moody convened in Northfield, Massachusetts, began in 1880 and were held annually until his death, though the first recording of the conferences, called *Northfield Echoes*, began only in 1894. Speakers at the Northfield conferences occasionally directed their addresses to Jewish themes. In 1894, a visitor from Palestine, Florence E. Ben Oliel, spoke at the conference. Ben Oliel was the daughter of Abraham Ben Oliel, a North African Jew who converted to Christianity around the middle of the nineteenth century and thereafter devoted his life to the evangelization of his brethren. In the 1890s, at the time of the conference, he was working as a missionary among the Jews of Jerusalem, where his daughter assisted him.[48] Ben Oliel's speech exhibited to some degree the role of converted Jews in the dispensationalist camp. Although she had converted to Christianity and was striving to evangelize Jews, she retained the ethnic identity of a Jew and looked favorably on the early beginnings of Jewish attempts at national restoration. Ben Oliel, therefore, rejoiced at the Zionist resettlement of Palestine, which was taking place before her eyes.[49]

Like other premillennialists, she saw this development as part of God's plans for humanity. Ben Oliel pleaded with her audience to do their utmost to help missionary work among the Jews. Her terminology reflects a prevalent notion among premillennialists, namely that missionary work among the Jews is an expression of kindness toward that nation and the repayment of indebtedness Christians owe to God's chosen people. Opposing the traditional Christian view, Ben Oliel claimed that the Jews had been God's messengers to spread his Word. Christians, however, had repaid them by overtaking God's promises to themselves.[50]

Jews who converted to Protestant Christianity out of religious conviction in the nineteenth and twentieth centuries have often been attracted to premillennialism. Some have even played leading roles in the premillennialist movement and many have been active in the field of missions to the Jews.

Those who converted to premillennialism were not embarrassed by their Jewish background. The dispensationalist belief offered them the opportunity to embrace Christianity and still see themselves ethnically as Jewish, allowing them to take pride in their Jewish roots. Few independent congregations of Christian Jews emerged in the nineteenth century. Some of them aimed at amalgamating the Christian belief with Jewish rites. This practice was not yet accepted by many premillennialists, most of whom considered Jews who had accepted Jesus as their Savior to have fully joined the body of the true Christian believers. Only in the 1970s did separate congregations of messianic Jews become normative among Jewish converts to evangelical Protestantism, as well as gain acceptance by the bulk of American premillennialists.

Other speakers at the 1894 conference also referred to the Jewish place in the eschatological times. George C. Needham, who delivered an address on the Second Coming of Jesus, expressed his opinion that, "The Jew shall be in exaltation. In opposition to their national degradation in the present age, the seed of Jacob are to take precedence in the age to come." The Jewish homeland, he promised, "shall be restored, redivided, and extended to the limits of the original grant to Abraham." Jerusalem, he believed, "shall become the ecclesiastical center of the world. . . . Ten men shall take hold of on a Jew and say 'We will go with you; for we have heard that God is with you.' "[51]

The American Colony in Jerusalem

In 1881, while the bulk of dispensationalist leaders in America were busy spreading the new belief, one activist of the movement, Horatio G. Spafford, settled with a small group of followers in Jerusalem.

Spafford was born in 1828 in North Troy, New York. He settled in Chicago in 1856 and became an affluent lawyer and real estate investor. In Chicago he was converted to dispensationalism and became a close associate of Dwight Moody as well as William Blackstone. In addition to his business engagements he devoted his time to evangelism, which included the promotion of the belief in the imminent return of Jesus. Spafford, his Norwegian-born wife Anna, and their four daughters, lived in the suburban neighborhood of Lake View. In 1873, the family decided to visit Europe. The ship in which they sailed, *Ville du Havre*, sank, and all four daughters drowned.[52] Misfortunes continued to befall the Spaffords. In 1880, their son, who was born after the *Ville du Havre* tragedy, died of scarlet fever.

The grief-stricken Horatio Spafford developed new theories concerning life after death. He began to believe in universal salvation and claimed that there was no devil and no hell, and that children, at any rate, would not be sent to hell. Spafford obviously wanted to believe that he would be reunited with his beloved children. As a result of what was considered heterodoxy, Spafford was expelled from the Presbyterian church on Fullerton Avenue where he had been a member for many years.

In 1881, the Spaffords and a group of friends who shared their views decided to go to Jerusalem. The trip was not a result of the dispensationalist belief the Spaffords and their followers shared. The excursion to Jerusalem and the settlement there manifested a quest for a spiritual remedy the Spaffords hoped to find for their agonized souls.[53]

Dispensationalism does not advocate the settlement of Gentile believers in Palestine. This task is designated for the Jews, who are expected to return there prior to the arrival of Jesus. Gentile believers are going to be raptured and meet Jesus in the air. In the millennial kingdom, when Jesus would rule the world from Jerusalem, the Jews would live in their land and carry out the Lord's administration. The Gentile nations would then live in their own lands. Except for missionaries who came to work among Jews, dispensationalists rarely made an effort to settle in Palestine. The Spaffords' experience was thus a unique one.

In Jerusalem, the American group led a communal life that they believed to be in line with the life led by the early Christian community in Jerusalem, as described in Acts. They first settled in the Moslem quarter in the Old City. Later on, they acquired a home in Nablus Road outside the city walls. The whole neighborhood was soon to be known as the American Colony. The group came to be at odds with the American consul in Jerusalem, Selah Merrill, who looked with suspicion on their religious beliefs and way of life, including the decision of the colony to practice celibacy.[54]

In 1896, a group of Swedes who had immigrated to America decided to move to the American Colony. They were joined by compatriots who immigrated directly from Sweden to Jerusalem. The American-Swedish community grew to more than 150 members. They engaged in various economic enterprises and also carried on impressive relief work among the poor of Jerusalem. The colony established a children's hospital, which they operated until the 1970s; a children's clinic was still operating in the late 1980s. The founders of the American Colony were instrumental in helping hundreds of Yemenite Jews who immigrated to Palestine in 1882 and arrived penniless in Jerusalem. They saw in the Yemenite immigration "a sign of the times" that indicated that the arrival of Jesus was imminent.[55]

While the Spaffords were considered heretics by the Presbyterians, their dispensationalist friends did not excommunicate them and continued to look favorably on them. Both William Blackstone, who visited Jerusalem in 1889, and Dwight Moody, who visited in 1892, paid visits to their old friends. The American settlement in Jerusalem, however, was not sponsored by the dispensationalist movement. The Spafford endeavor was conceived as a private enterprise.

The second generation of the American Colony did not hold to the religious convictions and messianic hopes that played such an important part in building the colony. After the death of Anna Spafford in 1923, factions split the community, whose new head was the Spaffords' daughter Bertha (b. 1878). A group of Swedes decided to split from the colony; others left Jerusalem altogether. An economic struggle developed between the rival parties. The American Colony as religious commune ceased to exist.[56] Membership in the colony continued to dwindle, and only a remnant of the descendants of the original American settlers remained in the city. Thereafter, the members of the American Colony interacted primarily with the Arab population in the city, and without the messianic hopes, the attitude of the second generation in the colony became hostile toward the Zionist cause.[57]

After the war of 1948 and the division of Jerusalem into Jewish and Arab parts, the American Colony found itself on the Jordanian side of the city. Living for nineteen years under Jordanian administration, the third generation of the colony welcomed the Israeli takeover of east Jerusalem in 1967.

The International Prophetic Conferences

Immigration to Jerusalem was the exception. The main concern of American dispensationalists was spreading their belief and building a movement of expectants of the end of time. One of the vehicles through which premillennialists operated was a series of what came to be known as International Prophetic Conferences. Held in the biggest halls of major American cities and attracting large audiences, the conferences helped to shape a more coherent and unified premillennialist creed. They were also an opportunity for American premillennialists to host and build contacts with their counterparts from abroad, especially from the English-speaking world.

The speeches delivered at the conferences reflect both the centrality of the Jewish people and the prospect of their restoration to Zion in the premillennialist creed and the striking ambivalence of the premillennialist attitude toward Judaism and Jews.

The first conference convened in New York in 1878 at the initiative of the Niagara Conference people. Although some premillennialists of the historicist school also presented their opinions, dispensationalism gave the convention its spirit. Many of the speeches were intended to defend the legitimacy and validity of the premillennialist creed. One of the ways this was done was by trying to prove the antiquity of the creed and its continuity throughout the ages.[58] William R. Nicholson, a bishop in the small Reformed Episcopal church, delivered a major speech on the Jewish role in the eschatological times. He claimed that the Bible prophesies "the gathering back of all the twelve tribes of Jacob from their dispersion, continued through so many ages, to their own covenanted land, Palestine, and the resettlement of them there as one nation." Nicholson insisted that biblical prophecies refer specifically to Israel in the flesh (the Jewish nation) and to the land of Israel (the country). He opposed symbolic or typologic interpretations that denied the literal one. Nicholson also rejected the notion that the prophecies for the regathering of Israel were fulfilled in the return of Jews from the Babylonian exile in the fourth century B.C.E.[59]

According to Nicholson, the return of the Jews to their land would take place in two phases, one preceding the return of Jesus to earth and the other following that event. The Jews would return to their land before accepting Jesus as their Lord.

> They would be gathered back in their unconverted state. . . . Previous to the coming of the Lord . . . it will be still as rejecters of Christ and rebellious to God, that they will occupy their land. And it is as speaking of them at that very time, that Isaiah ascribes to them pride and haughtiness, the loftiness of the cedars of Lebanon, and the stiff sturdiness of the oak of Bashan.[60]

After returning to their land, "They will have rebuilt their temple and reestablished their temple services, before the coming of their Lord. . . . The object of their gathering," he claimed, "is ultimately their conversion, but primarily, their chastisement and suffering. Their terrible suffering when ended will have reduced them to a remnant. 'The third part shall be brought through the fire, and be refined as silver is refined' (Zach. 13:9)."[61]

After the arrival of Jesus to earth, the Jews "will look on Him whom they have pierced . . . they shall mourn for their sins. . . . They will believe in the Lord Jesus Christ, and they shall be forgiven; not forgiven only, but accepted in all the preciousness of that Name which they and their nation had rejected and abhorred." As for the country itself, Nicholson believed that, "In extent it will be according to the covenant with Abraham. As to fertility and beauty . . . 'It shall blossom abundantly' . . . (Isaiah 35). . . . Great and exalted will be millennial Israel's position and influence in the earth," the speaker promised.[62] Nicholson's exposé manifests with sharp clarity the ambivalence in the dispensationalist attitude toward the Jews. On the one hand they are God's chosen nation to whom the biblical prophecies refer. They will be restored to their ancient land and serve as the central nation in the millennial kingdom. On the other hand, as they have refused to recognize Jesus as their Messiah, their character reflects obnoxiousness and rebellion. Their road to glory is paved with suffering and destruction.

In November 1886, the advocates of premillennialism convened a second International Prophetic Conference, this time in Chicago. This conference was already dominated almost completely by the futurist, dispensationalist school of eschatology. Like all the International Prophetic Conferences, it attracted large crowds of interested listeners.

A few speakers discussed the Jewish people and their role in the drama at the end of this age. Nathaniel West, a Presbyterian minister from St. Paul, Minnesota, who was one of the earliest converts to dispensationalism in America,[63] delivered a speech entitled "Prophecy and Israel." He expressed his opinion on the centrality of the nation of Israel in God's plan for the redemption of humanity. "A predetermined plan lies at the foundation of the whole evolution of God, in which Israel appears as an abiding factor. The fortunes of the chosen people decide the fortunes of the world . . . 'salvation is from the Jews.' " He proposed that just as at the end of the Mosaic age, Israel formed the historic basis of the New Testament "church," at the end of this present age, Israel would form the historic basis for the New Testament "kingdom."[64]

In his view, Israel fulfills the same function of salvation for humanity as the Messiah does.

Israel stands in prophecy, as in history, the elect agent of salvation, in a national sense, as truly as does the Messiah in a personal sense, each a "Son of God," and is identified so closely with Messiah Himself, both in suffering and glory, as the

"Servant of Jehovah." . . . Israel and Messiah, though historically separated now, are indissolvably united, as mediators and bringers of salvation to the world the one nationally, the other personally, alike in their humiliation and glory.[65]

West thus saw an additional meaning in the suffering and humiliation of the Jewish people. They are those of "the Suffering Servant." They are part of the troubles the messenger of redemption undergoes in his mission of salvation. Like many other dispensationalists who dealt with the theme of Israel in prophecy, he devoted large portions of his speech to countering the prevailing Christian views that identified the church with Israel and Canaan with Christendom.[66] Quoting from the Scriptures to validate his claims, West manifested in his presentation a strong element of apology and defense of dispensationalist biblical hermeneutics, apology that reflected the novelty of dispensationalism and its outlook on Israel in the Protestant camp.

In his speech, William J. Erdman, minister of a Congregational church in Boston and one of the leading activists of the first generation of dispensationalists in America, interpreted Romans 11: 25-27, in which Paul discussed the future of the Jewish nation.[67] In Erdman's view, Paul's words "set forth the grounds of the mysterious dealings of God with Israel and the gentiles in this present time." He used Romans 11 to combat the traditional Christian understanding of Israel's role in history. Erdman claimed that Paul's announcement of "this mystery" was intended, among other purposes, "to prevent the self-complacent conceit of believers from among the Gentiles that, because of the fall of Israel there was for them, as a nation no future of special blessing and pre-eminence. This warning against gentile high mindedness is still most pertinent and necessary." Although defending the position of Israel against the attempts by Christians to deny the Jews their role in history, Erdman spoke harshly about the Jewish unwillingness to accept Jesus' messiahship. His criticism of Israel and his insistence on the eminent place of the Jews as God's chosen people were interwoven. "Israel, though now as a people smitten with Judicious hardness of heart shall again be restored to the favor and blessing."[68]

In December 1895, a third International Prophetic Conference took place in Allegheny, Pennsylvania. Ernest F. Stroeter, from the Hope of Israel mission in New York, delivered a major address regarding the place of the Jewish nation in the premillennial understanding of God's plan and purpose in the ages. By 1895, dispensationalists in America had become engaged in aggressive missionary work among the Jews. Stroeter's address came, among

41

other things, to promote the ideology of his particular mission in an attempt to influence others to accept its line. Other speakers in the conference also referred to the Jewish nation and its role in God's plans for humanity in their speeches.

In his speech, J. A. Owens, a Methodist minister from New Jersey, discussed the dispensationalist understanding of the present age, referring to "the times of the Gentiles" as an "awful gap" or a "break in the predestined thread of Israel's history." However, in spite of this break, Owens declared, "God's gifts to Israel of the land and of earth pre-eminence among the nations (Gen 12:2, 3; Gen 27:29; Numb 28:9, etc.) and the calling [of Israel to be a prophetic priest-king nation under the Messiah] is without repentance . . . (Rom 11:28, 29) . . . the present gap . . . shall be followed by a glorious fulfillment of Jehovah's promise to their fathers."[69]

Both William G. Moorehead, a professor of New Testament at the United Presbyterian Seminary at Xenia, Ohio, and Edward P. Goodwin, pastor of the First Congregational Church of Chicago, emphasized the strong ties between the way the premillennialists understood themselves as biblical literalists and how they perceived the Jews as God's chosen nation, and as such, the object of the biblical prophecies for Israel at the end of days. Moorehead complained, "If we spiritualize it, and substitute some other place for Jerusalem and some other place for Israel, then we may adjust it to any event we please, may make it mean whatever we wish."[70] Goodwin asked, "By what principle, then, can the exegetical dagger be made to stab the literalness . . . so that there shall be no throne of David, no literal reign; no literal house of Jacob?" He said further,

> It is therefore the clear necessity of the Scripture teaching as to the resurrection that our Lord's return should be literal, personal, visible . . . that "they that pierced Him shall look upon Him," and that He shall "come as the Redeemer to Zion," take the "throne of David" and "reign over the house of Jacob forever" (Matt 25:30; Rev 1-7; Zach 12:10; Is 59:20; Luke 1:23).[71]

Dispensationalism is based, among other things, on the idea that God's plans for humanity are revealed in the Bible. Premillennialists insisted, therefore, on the inerrancy of the Bible as the word of God. Premillennialism was spreading in America during the years when the debate over the higher criticism of the Bible versus the insistence on the inerrancy of the Scriptures had become a live issue in the American Protestant camp, contributing to the emerging division between conservatives and liberals. The premillennialist movement associated itself more and more with the conservative elements in American Protestantism. Dispensationalists were among the vigorous leaders of the emerging fundamentalist movement, combating modernist notions they believed were stripping the Bible of its meaning and purpose.

The strong link that developed between premillennialism and conservative-evangelical Protestantism in America helped spread the belief in the Second Coming. American evangelists have often sold their audiences a package deal of regeneration that combined the belief in the imminent return of Jesus with a conservative outlook on Christianity. The dispensationalist hope has often been accepted as part of a broader outlook on Christian life and as an offspring of the conception of Scripture as divine and inerrant. It was as part of this deal that many of the millions of Americans who came to believe in the Second Coming accepted the idea of the central role the Jewish nation was to play in Jesus' arrival and in the millenial kingdom.

The fourth International Prophetic Conference was held in December 1901 in the Clarendon Street Baptist Church in Boston, Massachusetts. The international character of the conference was evident: half the speakers came from outside the United States, from Britain and Canada. In this conference, as in the previous ones, speakers referred to the role of the Jewish people in God's plans for humanity as understood by dispensationalist biblical hermeneutics.

Sir Robert Anderson, an Englishman, sent a letter that was read in the conference. Anderson's words express the connection that dispensationalists made between their eschatological hope, the acceptance of the Jews as "Israel," and the opposition to the higher criticism of the Bible.

A noted teacher of the generation now passed away once told me that the crisis of his Christian life was caused by a remark let drop by a friend with reference to Isaiah XI:12. Though not only a Christian but a theologian and a scholar (he had been a Fellow of his college at Oxford), he knew nothing of prophecy, and needed to learn that in Scripture "Israel" meant Israel, and "Judah" meant Judah, and that God intended to restore that nation to prosperity and blessing. The Bible became a new book to him; and from being a mere country parson he became a teacher of teachers. And I desire to bear testimony to the help which the study of prophecy has been to me personally. Five and twenty years ago it helped to save me from the "Higher Criticism."[72]

Note that both Anderson and the scholar to whom the writer of this testimony refers first accepted the dispensationalist eschatological belief and consequently rejected the higher criticism.

William G. Moorehead this time gave a laudatory speech concerning the role of the Jewish people as God's chosen nation.

> "The Jews, your Majesty," was the pertinent reply of the believing courtier when Frederick the Great asked him for the credentials of the Bible. If I were asked to furnish proof of the world's conversion, of evidence that God will one day bring this whole planet in subjection to himself, and fill it with his glory, as he has promised, I should unhesitatingly point to Israel, the chosen people, the center for blessing for the whole world.[73]

Like many dispensationalists, Moorehead believed that evangelization of the Jews was a sign of love and thankfulness toward them, and he complained about the Christian maltreatment of the Jews. Neglect on the part of Christians to engage more aggressively in the evangelization of the Jews was part of his complaint.

> We look in vain for any extensive and loving evangelization of the Jews . . . the darkest and saddest page of the Church's history is . . . not only obstinate neglect of the Jew, but contempt for him, and hatred and oppression and spoliation and expulsion and attempted extermination by the so called Christian nations.[74]

Moorehead—who so much valued the place of the Jews in bringing about salvation to the world and who defended vehemently this view against other scriptural hermeneutics—had little appreciation for Judaism. According to his view it was based on erroneous interpretations of the Old Testament.

> . . . one of the striking things to be witnessed in modern Jews, no less than in those of remote times, is their inability to understand the Old Testament. They cannot see its truth, nor grasp its real meaning, for Christ is its key, and rejecting him, they have lost the key, and so their own Scriptures are to them an insoluble enigma.[75]

Moreover, while the speaker had no doubt as to the glory that awaited the Jews in the future, in this dispensation ("the times of the Gentiles") "by their unbelief, their rejection of the Messiah, they have lost their proper place in the

Kingdom, and are fallen from the high dignity and noble privileges that belong to them."[76]

The future of the Jewish people at the time of the Great Tribulation and the millennial kingdom also occupied the bulk of James Gray's address to the conference as well as a large part of that of Leander W. Mundhall of Germantown, Pennsylvania. Mundhall's view presented a twofold perception of the fate of the Jews. "They were forgetful and disobedient; and to this day, they are scattered and peeled—a sad, weary, and wandering people. But it will not always be so."[77]

William J. Erdman presented an analysis of the Book of Isaiah. Erdman viewed it as one entity written by one prophet and divided into two parts. According to his view, the second part of Isaiah (chaps. 40-66) included a detailed description of Jewish history during the current dispensation ("the times of the Gentiles"). He explored that history, concluding with a description of Israel in the millennial kingdom, when "Jerusalem, redeemed, exalted, sovereign, [will be] the source and center of Universal power, law and worship, the praise and joy of the whole earth."[78]

Sholto D. C. Douglas, from Scotland, described the role of Antichrist in the events that would take place, according to dispensationalist belief, at the time of the Great Tribulation. Antichrist, the speaker believed, was probably a Jew who would make a covenant with the Jews who, "Having . . . returned in part to their own land will, whilst in unbelief, rebuild their temple and institute sacrifice."[79]

The Fifth International Prophetic Conference took place at the Moody Bible Institute, in Chicago, in February 1914. Speakers again referred to the Jewish people and to the prospect of their return to Palestine. But for the first time in prophetic conferences, a speaker commented on the rise of the Zionist movement, which premillennialists had for some time enthusiastically regarded as a "sign of the times" indicating the imminent return of Jesus. In his address, William B. Riley, minister of the First Baptist Church, Minneapolis, who later established the Northwestern Bible School, said:

> The Zionist movement of recent years has impressed profoundly many students of the Scriptures. It has looked to them like the beginnings of fulfillment for that great line of prophecies that point unmistakably to the return of the Jew to his native land, and the making of Jerusalem ready for Israel's King.[80]

The conference held a few symposia, one of which was dedicated to "The Lord's Coming in Relation to Israel." At that symposium only two speakers delivered addresses. The first was by Arno C. Gaebelein, and the address following was by Charles A. Blanchard, president of Wheaton College. Gaebelein devoted most of his speech to the role of Israel in the past and present ages, prior to the eschatological events that are yet to occur.[81] Blanchard, on the other hand, concentrated on the prospect for the Jewish nation in the future, in the Great Tribulation and in the millennial kingdom. Between the two of them they covered most aspects of the dispensationalist understanding of the history and future of Israel.

American dispensationalists were deeply impressed by the events of World War I, its unprecedented magnitude in the history of wars, and the turmoil and destruction it brought along with its results, one of which was the British conquest of Palestine. Inspired by the world events, which fueled the dispensationalists with a sense of righteousness concerning their interpretation of the course that history was taking, they convened two prophetic conferences in 1918.

The first conference took place in Philadelphia in May and references were made at it to the rise of the Zionist movement and the British capture of Palestine. Albert E. Thompson, who served until the outbreak of World War I as pastor of the American Church in Jerusalem, described the capture of Jerusalem by the British as a "pivot in prophecy." He expressed the view that the capture of the city of the great king means that the end of the desolation is at hand.[82] A similar attitude toward these events was expressed by P. W. Philpott, pastor of the Gospel Tabernacle of Hamilton, Ontario.[83]

The conference adopted a statement of faith, the fifth article of which read as follows: "We believe that there will be a gathering of Israel to her land in unbelief, and she will be afterward converted by the appearance of Christ on her behalf."[84]

The last International Prophetic Conference took place at Carnegie Hall, in New York, in November 1918. Two speakers, Reuben A. Torrey, dean of the Bible Institute of Los Angeles, and David J. Burrell, pastor of Marble Collegiate Church, New York, referred to the destruction that accompanied World War I as an indication that the premillennialist interpretation of world events was correct. It was proof that human society was not improving. On the contrary, the world situation was deteriorating. They viewed the war as a "sign of the times" that indicated that the end of the age was near and the eschatological time was at hand.[85]

Arno C. Gaebelein and William B. Riley saw in the capture of Jerusalem by the British also "a sign of the times" that indicated that history had reached its eschatological phase. "To the Jews it means that their hopes are about to be realized. To us true Christian believers it is the sign that the times of the Gentiles are rapidly nearing their close," Gaebelein asserted.[86]

Although dispensationalists awaited the Second Coming of Jesus, they saw themselves as good American patriots, participated in the war effort, and took pride in the American state. They portrayed America as a righteous nation (when compared to all the other nations). However, as worthy as her leaders might be, they could not offer long-lasting remedies to many of the world's evils. Only the arrival of Jesus, Riley claimed, could bring the desired universal peace.[87]

The addresses delivered at the International Prophetic Conferences reveal strong awareness on the part of the speakers of the novelty of the dispensationalist theories and the historical role these theories assigned to the Jews. The speeches defended the premillennialist beliefs and tried to show that such beliefs were based on sound interpretation of the Scriptures. As all the participants in the conferences were premillennialists who believed in the same eschatological scheme, they usually varied only in their emphasis on different aspects of the hermeneutical system they shared and in the biblical passages they quoted.

Throughout this period, dispensationalists gained more confidence in the correctness of their interpretation of the Bible and their understanding of history and its course. World War I helped validate their claim that the world situation was not improving (as postmillennialists had claimed). The rise of the Zionist movement, the British takeover of Palestine, and the Balfour Declaration became the verification par excellence that events indeed were preceding in accordance with the dispensationalist belief.

Analysis of the dispensationalist attitude toward the Jewish people as manifested in various speeches in the Prophetic Conferences reveals an attitude of striking ambivalence. On the one hand, speakers refer to the Jewish nation with appreciation and warmth that were almost unprecedented in the history of Christian relationship with Judaism. This approach naturally derived from the importance and prominence of the Jews in the events that would lead to the arrival of Jesus and in the eschatological times. However, the belief in the centrality of the Jewish people in God's plans for humanity did not eliminate the deep-rooted disappointment and anger that Christians often held toward the Jews for their refusal to accept Jesus as the Lord. Dispensationalists viewed postbiblical Judaism as an erroneous tradition and the Jewish nation therefore as living in the dark.

The Scofield Reference Bible *and* The Fundamentals

Prophetic conferences were not the only means dispensationalists used to express their eschatological conviction. A series of publications helped transform the premillennialist belief into a popular conviction accepted by millions of Americans. Many of the early theoreticians of the movement wrote books and pamphlets in which they propagated their eschatological hopes. The publication most instrumental in spreading dispensationalism in America was the *Scofield Reference Bible*, named after its commentator and editor Cyrus I. Scofield.

Scofield had served as a soldier in the Confederate Army during the Civil War. Later he worked as a lawyer until 1879, when a conversion experience made him adopt the dispensationalist hope and devote himself to the church. Scofield served as pastor of a Baptist congregation in Dallas, Texas, and of another in Northfield, Massachusetts. He participated in the Niagara and Northfield Bible study conferences and in the International Prophetic Conferences and became one of the influential leaders of the premillennialism movement in America. In 1909 his *Reference Bible* was published. About two million copies were sold in the three decades following its publication.[88]

The *Scofield Reference Bible* is the King James version of the Bible edited and accompanied by notes and commentaries. Scofield gave titles to the various chapters in the Scriptures as well as subtitles to parts within. Commentaries were printed at the bottom of the pages. In many of the books in the Bible the editor's work is not extremely apparent. However, he edited and commented much more aggressively in books that relate to prophecy, such as Daniel and Revelation.

The titles and subtitles with which he chose to precede the biblical text included an interpretation of their content that supported the dispensationalist eschatological understanding. The Scofield commentaries introduced the reader to dispensationalist terminology. They contained such terms as "the Great Tribulation," "the time of Jacob's trouble," "the time of the Gentiles," and "the pretribulation rapture." The dispensationalist idea of the future of the Jewish people was introduced to many homes in evangelical Protestant America through this biblical commentary and text.

To understand the rise of premillennialism to a position of influence and prominence among conservative American Protestants, one has to take into account another literary enterprise, *The Fundamentals*, which began to appear in 1910.[89]

In 1909, Lyman Stewart, an oil magnate from California and an active dispensationalist, had decided to sponsor a publication that would be devoted to combating the higher criticism of the Bible as well as other liberal-modernist trends that in his view threatened to undermine Christian beliefs. *The Fundamentals* were edited successively by Amzi C. Dixon, pastor of Moody Church in Chicago; Louis Meyer, a converted Jew who had abandoned the medical profession and became a minister and evangelist; and Reuben Torrey. Between 1910 and 1915 *The Fundamentals* appeared in twelve volumes, with three million copies distributed altogether. Articles were devoted to defending the belief in the inerrancy of the Bible as well as other elements of the Christian belief that were considered to be under attack by modernists, such as the virgin birth of Jesus and his resurrection. A whole volume was devoted to mission and evangelization. A few articles were dedicated to exposing what their authors considered to be the errors and dangers of misleading beliefs, such as Mormonism, Christian Science, Roman Catholicism, and socialism.

The editors of *The Fundamentals* were premillennialists, as were many of the participants in the editorial committee and the writers whose articles were published in the series. However, although the hope of the second return of Jesus echoes in the background of *The Fundamentals*, it is not presented openly very often in the content. Nonpremillennialists from the conservative camp in American Protestantism also wrote for *The Fundamentals*, and the need to unite in defending the fundamentals of Christianity prevented the premillennialists from turning the publication into a dispensationalist organ. Only one article explicitly expressed belief in the dispensationalist eschatological hope. Its author, Arno C. Gaebelein, intended to defend the inerrancy of the Bible. In his opinion, the history of the Jewish nation was proof of the absolute accuracy of the Bible. Numerous biblical prophecies had been fulfilled in the history of Israel.

> These oracles of God, the Holy Scriptures, the Law and the Prophets, are filled with a large number of predictions relating to their own history. Their unbelief, the rejection of the Messiah, the results of that rejection, their dispersion into the corners of the earth, so that they would be scattered among all the nations,

the persecutions and sorrows they were to suffer, the curses which were to come upon them, their miraculous presevation as a nation.

Other prophecies, like the restoration of the Jews to their land, were expected to occur in the future.[90]

The Fundamentals helped to promote premillennialists to leadership in the emerging fundamentalist camp. Many of the outstanding spokesmen of American fundamentalism (a term that was derived from *The Fundamentals*) have been vigorous premillennialists. The connection between premillennialism and fundamentalism has often been so strong that Ernest Sandeen, author of a history of the premillennialist movement in America, saw the two phenomena as almost identical and reached the erroneous conclusion that premillennialism was indeed the core and root of the fundamentalist movement.[91]

Nevertheless, the support of Zionism and the state of Israel on the basis of eschatological beliefs has been deeply implanted in American fundamentalism, and although premillennialists by no means make up the entire evangelical-conservative camp in American Protestantism, their influence in shaping the political standpoint of this segment of American society has been so strong that conservative Protestants have, by and large, adopted a pro-Zionist line.

The Bible Institutes

While American premillennialists from 1875 to 1918 were operating through Bible and prophecy conferences, they created another vehicle to spread their message: the Bible institutes. The Bible institutes were established as training schools for evangelists: ministers, missionaries, Sunday school instructors, as well as interested laymen. They have also served as centers for such evangelical efforts as the spreading of the belief in the Second Coming of Jesus. The Bible institutes published periodicals that have served as major pulpits from which dispensationalists could express their views. The deans and presidents of these institutions were among the noted spokesmen and theoreticians of American premillennialism. In their writings they expressed many of the dispensationalist ideas concerning the Jewish nation and the prospect of its restoration to Palestine. Later on, from the 1930s, new premillennialist educational centers such as the Dallas Theological Seminary became leading forums for presentation of the dispensationalist belief and its attitude towards the Jews.

In 1886 the first Bible institute, the Chicago Evangelical Society, was established. After Moody's death in 1899, the name of the school was changed to the Moody Bible Institute. In its one hundred years of existence this institute has instructed more than 100,000 trainees, both men and women, in programs of study. Hundreds of thousands studied in the Correspondence School of the Institute. Besides courses on the Bible, the school prepares students for evangelization work as missionaries either abroad or at home. An additional part of the curriculum has been the study of eschatology and the defense of the inerrancy of the Bible.

The Moody Bible Institute has taken special interest in the evangelization of the Jews. In 1917, the institute established a special department to train missionaries for that purpose. The new interest they found in the Jewish people encouraged dispensationalists to engage in aggressive missionary work among what they considered to be God's chosen people. From the late 1880s to the early 1900s, numerous missionary enterprises with dispensationalist inclinations were established in major American cities.[92] The missionaries who devoted themselves to evangelization among Jews were confronted with problems they did not face when they attempted to spread the Gospel among the nonchurched Gentiles, for Jews, as a rule, rejected the attempts to Christianize them. The department in the Moody Bible Institute, therefore, was intended to provide special training to missionaries working in that particular field of Christian evangelism. The training included fieldwork and students were engaged in actual missionary work in the Jewish neighborhoods of Chicago, which, among other things, provided them with a firsthand experience of the animosity of the Jewish community toward missionaries.[93]

Numerous articles on missions to the Jews, the Jewish settlement in Palestine, and the Zionist movement appeared in the Moody Bible Institute Magazine, *The Institute Tie*, whose name was changed to *The Christian Workers Magazine* and, in 1920, to *The Moody Bible Institute Monthly*.[94] Reuben A. Torrey, the first superintendent of the institute, included the belief in the restoration of Israel to Palestine and in the Jewish nation's central role in the return of Jesus to earth in instructional books and articles he wrote on the Bible and on Christian doctrine.[95] Students at the Bible Institute were asked to study statements regarding these views as well as the biblical passages that were thought to substantiate them.

The statements dealt mostly with the glorified future that awaited the Jews in the messianic age. Among the purposes of and results to be expected from Christ's Second Coming Torrey included:

> Jesus Christ is coming again to deliver Israel in the day when his trials and suffering shall culminate. . . .
> Jesus Christ is coming again to gather together the outcasts of Israel from the East country and the West country and into Jerusalem. . . .
> Jesus Christ is coming again to deliver Israel and turn away ungodliness from Jacob. . . .
> At the Coming Again of Jesus Christ divided Israel-Ephraim and Judah—shall be reunited into one nation under one king David-Jesus. . . .
> Because of the Coming Again of Jesus Israel shall be cleansed from all their filthiness and all their idols, a new heart will be given them and a new spirit put within them. The stony heart shall be taken away from them and they given a heart of flesh. God will put His Spirit within them and cause them to walk in His statutes and they shall keep His judgments and do them. . . .
> Because of the Coming Again of Jesus Christ Israel shall be greatly exalted above the nations.[96]

Torrey's views concerning the future that awaited Israel before and after the Second Coming of Jesus reflect the dispensationalist ambivalence. On the one hand, the dean of the institute instructed his students that in the millennial kingdom "Israel shall be greatly exalted above the nations." On the other hand, Jesus is coming to "turn away ungodliness from Jacob." "Israel shall be cleansed from all their filthiness and from all their idols . . . the stony heart shall be taken away from them." The terminology the author used was taken from the biblical passages that dealt with the sinning sons of Israel.

The Jews' sin in latter times, so it seems, was their refusal to recognize Jesus as their Lord and Savior. Torrey also referred implicitly to the turmoils the Jews would witness at "the time of Jacob's trouble." He wrote, "Jesus Christ is coming to deliver Israel in the day when his trials and suffering shall culminate."

In 1908, Torrey decided to resign his position in the Bible Institute in order to devote himself completely to evangelistic campaigns. From 1912 to 1925, he served as dean of the Bible Institute of Los Angeles, at which time he participated in the editing of *The Fundamentals*. The ambivalent tone remained part of Torrey's projection of the fate of the Jews at the end of days. In a book he wrote during this period, *The Return of the Lord Jesus*, he stated, "But as great as their joy shall be, it shall begin with a great mourning,

mourning over their sin, and especially over their former rejection of their king." The author further discussed the suffering that would befall the Jews in the days that preceded the return of Jesus to earth. He continued with an elaborate description of the magnificent future Israel shall witness in the millennial kingdom.[97]

James M. Gray succeeded Torrey as director of the Moody Bible Institute. He was dean and later president of the institute, until he retired in 1934, a year before his death. Gray's attitude toward the Jewish people and Zionism provides another striking example of the ambivalence that characterized the premillennialist attitude.

On the one hand, Gray firmly believed that the Jewish nation was God's chosen nation, whose covenant with God was still valid and effective.[98] He expressed appreciation for what he considered the excellent achievements of Jews and for their contribution to society.[99] He was convinced of the glorious future that awaited Israel in the millennial kingdom. He responded to the Zionist movement, the Jewish immigration to Palestine, and the British overtaking of Jerusalem with great enthusiasm.[100] On the other hand, Gray, like other dispensationalists, also held some traditional Christian views. He believed that the Jews in biblical times had failed "to be faithful witness to Jehovah before the other nations of the earth, and in consequence is suffering the dispersion and persecution which, alas! we know about today."[101] Like many premillennialists, Gray denounced anti-Semitism and spoke against maltreatment of the Jews. At the same time he expressed his opinion that the Old Testament prophets had worse things to say about the Jews than modern anti-Semites.[102]

In the early 1920s the *Protocols of the Elders of Zion*, which supposedly revealed an international Jewish conspiracy to overtake the world, was circulated in America through the efforts of Henry Ford, Sr.[103] Gray was worried that the *Protocols* would inspire anti-Semitic outbursts, but nevertheless thought it likely that the document was authentic.[104] It is obvious that with Gray as well as among other dispensationalists, old prejudices against Jews were still alive. His messianic hope ensured an impressive amount of good will on his part toward Jews. He vehemently opposed the victimization of that nation. However, as the Jews did not yet accept Christ, they were capable of committing infamous acts and deeds of various sorts, including the conspiracy that the forgers of the *Protocols* accused them of conducting.

Bible institutes similar in character to the Moody Bible Institute, but not as prominent, were established in other cities in the United States. Two major

Bible schools were the Bible Institute of Los Angeles (BIOLA), established in 1903, and the Philadelphia School of the Bible, organized in 1914. Both schools have become Bible colleges offering undergraduate degrees. Both have also opened departments for training missionaries to the Jews.

William L. Pettingill, who in 1914 became the first dean of the Philadelphia School of the Bible, was the author of a few books of premillennialist teaching, in which he discussed the dispensationalist understanding of the place of Israel in God's plans for humanity. In 1905, he had published *Israel—Jehovah's Covenant People*, which was devoted entirely to popularizing the dispensationalist view of the Jewish people. The book was distributed among the Jews for missionary purposes. It describes in laudatory terms the glorified future that awaits the Jewish nation after its restoration to Palestine and the arrival of Jesus. In addition to predicting Israel's future when regathered in Palestine, Pettingill also denounced the ungrateful and hostile attitudes Christian nations have shown the Jews.[105]

In other tracts, Pettingill described the future of the Jewish people in a more complicated and ambivalent manner. On the one hand, he elaborated the details of Israel's magnificent future in the millennial kingdom. On the other hand, he mentioned the "time of Jacob's trouble" that awaited the Jews in the period that would precede the arrival of Jesus to earth and the treaty that they would, according to his belief, make with Antichrist. This treaty, he asserted, would result from the sad fact that the Jews had not yet accepted Jesus as their Savior. "The wholesale return of Jehovah's chosen people to their land will be preceded by the return of a remnant in unbelief. I say 'in unbelief,' because only unbelievers would be so deceived by the Beast king as to make a treaty with him."[106] Pettingill's words manifested a dispensationalist outlook that asserted that although the Jews were God's chosen nation, as they have not yet accepted Jesus as their Savior, they were living in a spiritual darkness and were therefore capable of committing grave crimes and errors. The glorified future that awaited the Jews in the millennial kingdom would take place after their conversion. In the meantime they were spiritually and morally deprived.

FOUR

The Zionist and Missionary Activity of William E. Blackstone

On March 5, 1891, a petition was presented to Benjamin Harrison. In it the president was requested to take steps that would lead to the restoration of Palestine to the Jews.

> To this end we respectfully petition His Excellency, Benjamin Harrison, President of the United States, and the Honorable James Blaine, Secretary of State, to use their good offices . . . to secure the holding at an early date of an international conference to consider the condition of the Israelites and their claims to Palestine as their ancient home, and to promote, in all other just and proper ways, the alleviation of their suffering condition.[1]

The petition was signed by 413 eminent Americans, among them Melville W. Fuller, chief justice of the United States; Congressman William McKinley from Ohio; William H. Russell, governor of Massachusetts; Hugh J. Grant, mayor of New York City; Edwin H. Fitler, mayor of Philadelphia; Robert R. Hitt, chairman of the House Committee on Foreign Affairs; T. B. Reed, speaker of the House of Representatives; James Cardinal Gibbons, archbishop of Baltimore; J. Pierpont Morgan; John D. Rockefeller; and Cyrus McCormick.

The initiator of the petition, William E. Blackstone, was a dispensationalist-premillennialist who was convinced that the return of the Jews to their land would precede the coming of Christ to earth. The submission of this petition marked a peak in his lifelong activity in favor of the Jewish restoration to Palestine. He was unique among early dispensationalists in America in his attempt to turn the premillennialist hopes concerning the return of the Jews to their land into reality. His efforts toward the establishment of a Jewish commonwealth in Palestine by means of international consent antedated the rise of political Zionism.

William E. Blackstone—The Man

William Eugene Blackstone was born on October 6, 1841 in Adams, Jefferson County, New York.[2] He was a descendant of Sir William Blackstone, the prominent eighteenth-century English jurist. Blackstone's father, however was a tinsmith, and Blackstone described his origins as "humble." His parents, Andrew and Sally Blackstone, were members of the local Methodist church. Blackstone's "conversion" (or "regeneration"), which he considered a major event in his life, occurred when he was ten years old, at a Methodist revival meeting in his hometown.[3]

Revival meetings were held all through the nineteenth century, occupying an important place in the religious atmosphere of the United States, especially in the newly settled areas of the country. Some major Protestant denominations, the Baptists, the Presbyterians, and especially the Methodists took part in the revivals and flourished along with them. The practical aim of the revivalists was to recruit new church members. On the spiritual level, revival meetings were designed to bring the "lost sheep" (unchurched) to Christ. The revivalists intended to make their audiences realize their sinfulness and their hopeless spiritual situation and the urgent need to repent and seek forgiveness. The inner struggle of the participants would culminate in a decision to accept Christ and his salvation. This inner act of "conversion" or "regeneration" was declared openly and solemnly. Henceforth, the newly converted should lead a life of holiness and become a devout member of the church for the rest of his life. In a highly emotional atmosphere that did not lack scenes of hysteria, people would step out and publicly declare their sinfulness and their acceptance of Christ and the opening of a new phase in their lives.[4] Blackstone's conversion occurred in such an atmosphere. He knew, so he wrote many years later, that his conversion was genuine, because he then went to his mother and confessed to her that he had stolen a small sum of money from her pocketbook.

Blackstone remained a Methodist for the rest of his life. Even when the Methodist church had taken a course that seemed to him too "modernist," he did not abandon his ties. Although Blackstone never received any official training as a minister, he served as a lay Bible teacher, preacher, and superintendent of a Sunday school. His formal title was lay exorcist, a title that does not exist in the Methodist church anymore.[5]

Blackstone never attended a college or a seminary. He was not an intellectual or an academician. Blackstone nevertheless wrote, published, and edited extensively. He corresponded a great deal with prominent public figures in a style that would not have embarrassed a well-educated person. In his writings Blackstone exhibited a wide knowledge of the Scriptures. His reading (when he found time for it) covered many areas of interest.[6] But, unlike his premillennialist friend Arno C. Gaebelein, he was not an autodidact. The scope of his knowledge and intellectual horizons were more limited.

During the Civil War, Blackstone tried to enlist as a combat soldier in the Union Army but was rejected on account of frailness. He then volunteered to serve in the army in the Christian Commission (an organization similar to the YMCA or the Red Cross). He was stationed in General Grant's headquarters.

On June 5, 1866, Blackstone married Sarah Louis Smith, who came from an affluent family. Some time after her father's death, his estate, which amounted to $125,000, was given to Blackstone to administer as a fund for the support of evangelical and missionary activity. It appears that the Blackstones led a happy life. His wife shared his religious convictions and was supportive of his work. They had two sons and a daughter. Blackstone's younger son spent most of his adult years as a missionary in China and Blackstone visited him there. Blackstone was especially attached to his daughter, Flora. Her death while a student at Oberlin College, shortly before her graduation, was a severe blow.

During the early years of their marriage, the Blackstones resided in Rockford, Illinois, where Blackstone sold agricultural insurance. In 1870 the family moved to Oak Park, west of Chicago, which was to be their home for more than forty years.

Blackstone's belief in the Second Coming of Christ had been piqued in his hometown when he heard a Presbyterian minister, Dr. Lord, preach a sermon on the subject. However, it was during his years as a businessman in Chicago that he acquired his premillennialist-dispensationalist belief. Others in Blackstone's social circle had been exposed to dispensationalism and some of his close friends shared his convictions. One was the lawyer, real estate investor, and evangelist Horatio G. Spafford, who was to found the American Colony in Jerusalem in 1881. Blackstone became associated with some of the leading protagonists of dispensationalism in America, men such as Dwight L. Moody and James H. Brookes. Blackstone became more and more a propagator and an evangelist of the dispensationalist belief. He lectured in churches and YMCAs, and used his business travel to try to convince the people he met of the truth of the imminent return of Christ.

In 1878, Blackstone decided to quit his business activity and devote himself to his evangelistic campaign. He explained this move in terms of a religious-mystical experience in which he was responding to God's call.[7] Although Blackstone henceforth devoted his time to his evangelistic endeavors, he did not give up his investments, and he continued to keep a close eye on his money and property. Blackstone was not the first successful businessman to give up his business activity in favor of evangelistic activity. Twenty years earlier, Dwight Moody had left the life of commerce to become America's leading evangelist.

Jesus is Coming

Blackstone saw a need for published material that could be distributed to people he met and whom he tried to persuade of the nearing coming of Christ. At first Blackstone approached his fellow dispensationalist friends, Horatio G. Spafford and James H. Brookes, and asked them to write the desired tract. Receiving a negative answer, he wrote it himself. This was followed by a second pamphlet on the same topic. The two small booklets were distributed as part of the propagation of the dispensationalist endeavor. In 1878, Blackstone rewrote these two booklets into a single volume entitled *Jesus is Coming*.[8] The 96-page book was to be Blackstone's most celebrated publication, which was revised and enlarged twice. The second edition, of 160 pages, was published in 1888, and the third edition, consisting of 256 pages, in 1908. In the first few decades of its circulation *Jesus is Coming* became one of the most popular books of dispensationalist teaching in America. It was translated over the years into forty-two languages, including Yiddish and Hebrew.

Blackstone's name did not appear in the book. He used his initials, W.E.B., as a pseudonym. Although the name of the author was undoubtedly known in dispensationalist circles in America, this does teach us something about Blackstone's character. Although he was sometimes engaged in celebrated activities and had grandiose plans, Blackstone was a modest man seldom motivated by ego.

Though the modernist-conservative debate in America had not yet fully exploded when Blackstone published the first edition of his book, he clearly expressed in it his opinion against the higher criticism of the Bible.[9] Blackstone, like all dispensationalists, considered himself a biblical literalist. He criticized the spiritual understanding of the Bible and cut himself off from hermeneutical traditions that had been started by the fathers of the church. The only authority he recognized was the Bible. Again, like other dispensationalists, he did pay tribute to Martin Luther and the Reformation.

The Hebrew version of *Jesus is Coming*, published in 1925, carries a different title from the original English one. In Hebrew it is called *Hofaat Ha-Mashiach Ha-Shnia* (*The Second Appearance of the Messiah*). The book was intended for missionary purposes. The Jewish reader was expected to begin reading it before he had accepted Jesus as his Messiah. The name of Jesus was thus omitted from the book's title, possibly because it might have scared away some potential readers. Moreover, the Hebrew title stresses the fact that the Messiah had already come once before, while in the original title this point is taken for granted.

In the preface, the translator described Blackstone as a friend of the Jewish people and outlined his Zionist activities. This was done in order to make Blackstone and the dispensationalist teaching in general credible and make the reading more attractive to Jews. In the Hebrew version, therefore, Blackstone's full name appeared.

The name of the translator does not appear in the book, but it seems that it might have been a Jewish convert to Christianity who presumably came from an Orthodox background and received a thorough Jewish education. It is apparent, however, that the translator had no contact with the revival in Hebrew literature and language that had taken place in the nineteenth century or with the revitalized spoken Hebrew of his time. The people who might have read the Hebrew of the translation were mostly Orthodox Jews who had not been exposed to the secular and Zionistic trends of the Hebrew language of their time. In most cases, these people could have read the Yiddish edition; they did not need this singular Hebrew version. It is doubtful, therefore, whether many or even any Jews at all were persuaded to accept dispensationalist Christianity by reading this translation.

Blackstone had thousands of copies of his book in various languages stored in Petra in Trans-Jordan. His intention was that Jews who would flee there at the "time of Jacob's trouble" would be able to discover the truth, accept Christ, and save themselves.[10]

Jesus is Coming was written with clarity and strength. It should be viewed, to a large extent, not as Blackstone's original views concerning the idea of the Second Coming of Christ, but as a summary of the ideas and the message of the dispensationalist movement in America as a whole. Blackstone's hermeneutical and eschatological schemes very much follow closely John N. Darby's and almost paralleled those of his friend Cyrus I. Scofield, whose hermeneutical work on the Bible, which was published about thirty years after the appearance of the first edition of *Jesus is Coming*, was to summarize and standardize the accepted mainline dispensationalist creed in America. Blackstone, on the whole, was not an original thinker, but a propagator of ideas. His main contribution was in his outstanding activity and initiatives as dispensationalist-evangelist, missionary, and supporter of Zionism. Blackstone, more than anyone else in America, tried to carry over into action what he considered the logical implications of his dispensationalist creed. This creed was not, however, his original innovation. The only original concept Blackstone introduced concerning his eschatological convictions was the idea that the United States had a special role and mission in the divine plan for humanity.

Jesus is Coming also includes a general evangelical approach. The unconverted reader had first, of course, to be converted to the belief in Jesus' divinity and to accept the meaning of Jesus' crucifixion and resurrection.[11] Blackstone, indeed, saw himself not merely as a propagator of dispensationalism but also as an evangelist and a missionary at large whose duty was spreading the Gospel and bringing people to Christ.[12] It is no wonder, therefore, that the book served for missionary purposes and was translated into so many languages. The Second Coming, according to Blackstone's message, makes the need for salvation urgent. People have to repent and convert soon or they might perish forever, should the great events begin before they have repented. The message of the imminent Second Coming, which occupies most of the book, is intended, among other things, to make the readers aware of this urgency. This is also the meaning and message of the title of the book, which implied that Jesus is coming again *soon*.[13]

The Place of the Jewish People in Blackstone's Eschatological Understanding

Blackstone, like all dispensationalists, considered the Jewish people the true heirs of biblical Israel and the object of biblical prophecies that refer to the reestablishment of the Davidic kingdom in the land of Israel. The more literal dispensationalist hermeneutics of the Bible resulted in the abandonment of the Christian claim to be the true Israel and the recognition of the Jewish nation as still playing a role in the course of history and fulfilling a purpose in God's plan for humanity.[14]

Blackstone considered the Jews' unwillingness to accept Jesus as their Messiah to have been a tragic mistake, one that had had devastating consequences for their fate ever since. It "has cost them centuries of sorrow."[15] It was because of the Jewish unwillingness to accept Jesus that his first appearance did not bring with it the establishment of the desired kingdom.[16] Blackstone refers to the Jewish maltreatment of Jesus as well as his crucifixion and killing. Like other dispensationalists of his day, he directs much of the blame for that on the Pharisees, perhaps in order to minimize the guilt of the Jewish people at large.[17] Blackstone should have known, however, that contemporary Judaism understands itself to be descended from the Pharisees, the holders of the "Oral Law."[18]

Although the Jewish people are scattered among the nations, Blackstone said, they had not been abandoned by God.[19] In the current dispensation, the sixth aeon, the Christian aeon, "the eon of mystery," or "the times of the Gentiles," the Jewish people have played a passive role in history, overshadowed by the church.[20] The current age, however, is considered a "parenthesis" in the advancement of the ages. In the very last period of this aeon the Jews have again resumed a major role in history, which is expressed by the Zionist movement and the new Jewish settlements in Palestine.[21]

In Blackstone's view, the millennial kingdom would be preceded by a period of seven years known as "the Great Tribulation." The body of believers in Christ would be raptured from earth, meet Jesus in the air, and remain with him there until he descends to earth. At that time, Israel, the Jewish nation, would undergo a period of turmoil known as "the time of Jacob's trouble."[22] The Jews would return to their land in "unbelief" and would reestablish a state, but this would not yet be the desired kingdom. Except for a minority, which would be persecuted by their own brethren, they would not accept Christ and would let themselves be ruled by Antichrist.

> . . . then the Lord shall come with his saints down to the earth and destroy this lawless Antichrist, deliver Israel, who will then look upon "him they have pierced." . . . He will judge the living nations and establish his millennial kingdom.[23]

In the last dispensation, the millennium, the Jewish nation, or more exactly, the part of the Jewish nation (about a third) that would survive the tribulation, would assume its place as the leading nation on earth, led by the son of David, Jesus the Messiah.

Blackstone expressed an appreciation for Orthodox Jews who, as a consequence of observing their old traditions, kept waiting for the Messiah, the fulfillment of the prophecies, and the reestablishment of their ancient kingdom in Palestine.[24] He saw Zionism as deriving from Orthodox Jews.[25] Blackstone, who took an interest in missionary work among the Jews, was probably also influenced in his attitude toward Orthodox, traditional Jews by the fact that they could be approached by missionaries and in a few instances would even convert to Christianity. The dispensationalist missionary efforts of which Blackstone was a major initiator were directed exclusively toward Orthodox Jews.

Though many Orthodox Jews instinctively rejected attempts to evangelize them, the dispensationalist messianic terminology that spoke about the appearance of "the Son of David" and the fulfillment of biblical prophecies was not strange to them. There was a common ground for discussion and persuasion.[26] In addition, Orthodox Jews were mostly immigrants who had just arrived from eastern Europe and were living in the poor sections of cities, making their living working in the sweatshops. Dispensationalist missions were located in the poor Jewish neighborhoods and the missionaries often approached Jews through relief work.

Blackstone occasionally published articles on Jewish religious themes in *The Jewish Era*, a magazine published by the Chicago Hebrew Mission. These articles reflected some of his ambivalence toward Judaism.[27] Blackstone believed that Judaism did not offer salvation and its adherents were doomed. Only in Christianity could Jews find true refuge and meaning. At the same time, Jewish tradition, the beliefs, laws, and rites of the Jewish people, kept them waiting for the Messiah and for the reestablishment of their old national home in Palestine. They were thus willing to fulfill the role intended for them in God's plan for human history.

By the same token Blackstone rejected Reform Judaism, as well as liberal, secular, or assimilated Jews in general. The major problem with Reform or secular Jews, so it seemed to Blackstone, was that they had turned their backs on their role in the divine plan for the end of days. They would not participate in the Jewish national restoration, which served as a means and preparation for the great events to come.[28] As these groups of Jews were unapproachable to dispensationalist missionary efforts and would not accept Christ, they would not be saved, either as Christians or as Jews in the land of Israel who would eventually accept Jesus in the course of the Great Tribulation. They would perish. Blackstone considered evangelical Protestant Christianity the only religious belief that offered salvation. Seculars, heathens, and non-Christians in general, as well as non-Protestant Christians or dissenting Protestant groups such as the Seventh-Day Adventists or the Mormons were doomed to perish.[29] Orthodox and Zionist Jews were in many ways an exception to this rule, an exception that derived from the fact that they fulfilled an important role as a means for the advancement of the millennial kingdom.

Blackstone was one of the least prejudiced against Jews among early dispensationalists. He did hold the sometimes popular conviction that Jews have an unusual gift for business and finance, that they are affluent, and that they are outstanding in their achievements.[30] There is no need to discuss the socioeconomic situation of the Jewish people in the late nineteenth and early twentieth centuries in order to prove that Blackstone's impression disregarded reality. One can find, however, almost no remarks in his writings that portray the Jews as greedy or malicious, or that attribute any other unpleasant characteristics to them. Such an attitude can indeed be found in the writings or sermons of some of Blackstone's fellow dispensationalists, such as Dwight Moody.

Blackstone also differs in this respect from his fellow dispensationalist missionary Arno C. Gaebelein. This difference in attitude toward the Jews reflects in part a difference in the temperament of these two early activists. Gaebelein's writings, especially in his later years, reflect not only opposition to the liberal and modernist trends of his time but also bitterness and anger, none of which characterized Blackstone, who was a man with an easy and friendly disposition. His writings and activity reflect strong conviction, but not anger. While some dispensationalist leaders like Gaebelein accepted the authenticity of the *Protocols of the Elders of Zion*, Blackstone expressed his conviction that the *Protocols* were forged documents and went out of his way to try to fight anti-Semitic propaganda. In a letter to the editor of Henry Ford's publication he wrote:

> In response to what you write about the publication in the *"Dearborn Independent,"* I would say I do not believe for a moment that the Jews have any organization for securing control of the government of the world, neither do I

believe that they were at all instrumental in the production or propagation of the so-called protocols, and it is amazing to me that such anti-semitic propaganda could be established in this country as well as in England.[31]

On a personal level, Blackstone established friendly relationships with Jews with whom he became acquainted through his Zionist initiatives, such as Nathan Straus and Louis D. Brandeis. In this respect, too, Blackstone was unique among dispensationalist leaders, who usually established social contacts only with Jews who had converted to dispensationalist Christianity.

Blackstone was aware that the audience he was trying to reach and persuade of the truth of dispensationalist convictions might reject the central place ascribed to the Jewish people in this premillennial eschatological scheme. He also knew that Christianity has traditionally denied the Jewish people the role of the "chosen people" ascribed to them in the Bible and claimed it for itself, and that many readers were brought up to believe that the role of the Jewish people in God's plans for humanity terminated with the emergence of Christianity. Blackstone was also aware of the prejudices that existed against Jews in the minds of many Christians.

> But, perhaps you say: "I don't believe the Israelites are to be restored to Canaan, and Jerusalem rebuilt."
> Dear Reader! have you read the declaration of God's word about it? Surely nothing is more plainly stated in the Scriptures. We would that we had space to quote the passages, but we can only give you a portion of the references. We beg of you to read them thoughtfully. Divest yourself of prejudice and preconceived notions, and let the Holy Spirit show you, from His word, the glorious future of God's chosen people, "who are beloved" (Rom. 11:28), and dear unto Him as "the apple of His eye" Zach. 2:8.[32]

Blackstone expected his audience to accept the idea that the Jews are indeed the true heirs of historical Israel to whom the biblical prophesies refer by asking them to read the biblical passages literally.

The claim to biblical literalism became one of the characteristics and part of the raison d'être for the fundamentalist movement that emerged in American Protestantism in the last decades of the nineteenth century and the first decades of the twentieth century in reaction to liberal trends known as "modernism."[33] It is in this segment of American culture that premillennialism is mostly to be found nowadays. Although not all fundamentalists adhere to the premillennialist conviction, there is a close link between the two phenomena. The idea of the central role of the Jewish people in the eschatological developments was accepted by millions of Americans as part of their acceptance of an eschatological conviction that in its turn was linked with a broad cultural and social perception, a cornerstone of which is an insistence on the inerrancy of the Bible and a claim to read the Bible literally.

Blackstone's Missionary Activity Among the Jews

Blackstone was the central figure in the establishment of the Chicago Hebrew Mission in 1887 and was one of the leaders of this mission for several decades, serving at times as its secretary-treasurer, superintendent, vice president, and editor of its magazine, *The Jewish Era*. The Chicago Hebrew Mission was organized along nondenominational lines. Although a number of mainline Protestant denominations, including the Episcopalian and several Lutheran churches, lent their hands to its establishment, its character was nevertheless clearly dispensationalist.[34] It seems that even nondispensationalist churches recognized the advantage of approaching the Jews with a dispensationalist message. As was mentioned, emphasis on the messianic hopes based on biblical prophecies, including the renewal of a national Jewish home in Palestine, appealed to Orthodox Jews.

The Jewish Era: A Christian Magazine on Behalf of Israel, published articles on the new Jewish settlements in Palestine, on the Zionist movement, on developments in world Jewry, on Jewish holidays and rites, as well as articles dealing with dispensationalist interpretations of biblical prophecies. The very name of the magazine implies a dispensationalist outlook on the division of human history, indicating that one era is that of the Jews. The subtitle is suggestive as well: the missionaries saw themselves as friends and helpers of the Jewish people. It also implies that the Jewish nation is not a rejected, wretched people whom the missionaries are to save by Christianizing, but a nation with a mission and purpose in the ages. The attempts at evangelization do not deny this mission, but rather emphasize and use it.

Dispensationalist missions, including Blackstone's Chicago Hebrew Mission, took an innovative approach. Formerly, Jewish converts to Christianity were supposed to Gentilize as well as Christianize. They were expected to turn their backs on their Jewish heritage and abandon all ties with the Jewish community. Their Jewish background was often regarded as a shameful disability that had to be overcome. The dispensationalists, on the other hand, emphasized the importance of the Jewish nation in the great events that would

65

precede the establishment of the millennial kingdom and its leading role in the millennial kingdom itself. The Jewish national restoration was looked on favorably and the overall attitude toward Jewish tradition was much more appreciative. The act of conversion was sometimes described not as a separation from Judaism but rather as an addition, as the true fulfillment of being a Jew.

Although many converts to dispensationalism in its earlier period chose to Gentilize, some continued to look on themselves as ethnically Jewish, manifested pride in their Jewish heritage, and showed interest in Jewish events.[35] Some attempts were made to continue the observance of some Jewish rites and customs. In a few instances, an attempt was even made to create a Christian-Jewish congregation. The Hope of Israel mission in New York under the leadership of Arno C. Gabelein and Ernest F. Stroeter in the years 1893-1899 tried to promote such an outlook. Similar attempts were also made outside the United States. In Toronto, S. B. Rohold presided over a Christian synagogue.[36] In Kishineff, Russia, Joseph Rabinowitz organized a Christian synagogue. He received help and encouragement from American dispensationalists, among them Blackstone.[37]

The attempt to amalgamate the belief in Jesus with a Jewish way of life did not meet with unanimous approval. In fact, debates over this issue have been going on in the dispensationalist camp ever since. Objections were made not only on the basis of the view that "in Christ there is no Jew or Greek," but also because of doubt over the question of how such attempts stand within the dispensationalist hermeneutical system, which differentiates between Jews and Christians and assigns them different roles in the course of history.[38] Blackstone did not speak out against the attempt to amalgamate Christianity and Jewish rites and to create a Judeo-Christian community, and he kept on good terms with Rabinowitz and with Rohold, who published regularly in *The Jewish Era*. He nevertheless made a sharp distinction between Christians and Jews in his dispensationalist scheme, considering Jews who had converted and accepted Christ to have completely joined the church, the body of believers, and to share the fate of their Christian brethren.[39]

Blackstone's involvement and efforts in the field of missions to the Jews raises a serious question: How do attempts to evangelize the Jews comport with the dispensationalist understanding of the role and future of this nation? If the Jewish nation is understood to play an important role in the end of days, in the events that precede the descent of Christ to earth, and in the millennial kingdom, why should it be Christianized? If the Jews are eventually going to accept Jesus as their Savior, why should Christian missionaries devote their energies to evangelizing them? Should they not direct those energies instead toward people of less fortunate nations who have no chance of salvation unless they accept Christ in this aeon? How could Blackstone be enthusiastic about the return of the Jews to their land and at the same time promote the preaching of the Gospel to the Jews?

The answer to these questions lies in part in the dispensationalist eschatological scheme. As mentioned, according to that belief, part of the Jewish people (about a third) would survive the Great Tribulation; the others would perish, never to rise from the dead, as is the fate of all Jews who die without accepting Christ. The Jews who would accept Jesus before the great eschatological events begin, on the other hand, would be raptured with all the true Christian believers and would thus be spared the misery of "the time of Jacob's trouble." Their salvation is guaranteed.[40] Should they die before the great events take place, they would rise from the dead.

In addition to this consideration that encouraged missionary zeal, dispensationalist missionaries acted on another major assumption. According to the dispensationalist eschatological scheme, 144,000 Jews would accept Jesus Christ as their Lord and Savior at the beginning of the Great Tribulation. These Jews would be persecuted by their brethren and some of them would be martyred. However, at the end of the Great Tribulation, the remnant of the Jewish people that would survive would recognize and accept Jesus as their Lord. They would be inspired by those Jews who had embraced Christianity at the beginning of the events. These Jews (144,000) would recognize the events as correlating with the Christian premillennial teachings they had learned while being exposed to dispensationalist missionary preaching and writing. They would be agents for spreading the Gospel and the truth of the messiahship of Jesus among the Jews in their time of trouble. The aim of the dispensationalist missions to the Jews was thus not merely to convert Jews at this time and age, but also to spread the knowledge and truth of the Gospel. It was necessary that there be 144,000 Jewish persons who would possess the knowledge of the Gospel (though they had not accepted it), so that they could fulfill their role at any moment the rapture might come and the Great Tribulation begin.

The dispensationalist mission to the Jews is based on the realistic assumption that only a limited number of Jews would convert.[41] The unconverted Jews would remain a large enough mass of people to fulfill their part in God's plan for humanity and get the eschatological scheme going.

Although the dispensationalist belief can rationally explain Blackstone's missionary efforts, one is still left with the impression that the attempt to evangelize Jews was almost an instinct to him. Blackstone was an outstanding initiator, founder, and activist in the field of Christian evangelism, both in America and abroad. He was among the founders of the Bible House in Chicago in 1889, whose name was changed in 1901, after Moody's death, to the Moody Bible Institute. Blackstone was also active in the founding of the Bible Institute of Los Angeles. He saw it as his special duty to help bring the Gospel to places where no missionary activities were being conducted. Blackstone, for example, was one of the founders, in 1887, of the International Missionary Alliance (later called the Christian and Missionary Alliance), whose original goal was "to carry the Gospel to Tibet and other unevangelized regions."[42] He applied to the Japanese authorities, pleading with them to secure the safe entrance of missionaries to that country.[43]

Blackstone considered the field of mission to the Jews a neglected one.[44] He tried to convince the American Protestant public of the need to spend more energy and resources on that enterprise. The eschatological hopes Blackstone developed toward the Jews and his interest in them made him especially eager to evangelize them. Although he had been engaged in other missionary endeavors, Blackstone considered his involvement in the attempt to evangelize Jews to be one of the great privileges and joys of his life.[45]

Blackstone was one of the few missionaries whom the Jews did not reject and despise. Zionist leaders in America kept close contacts with him. The only exception was Rabbi Bernhard Felsenthal from Chicago,[46] who supported Blackstone in his pro-Zionist initiatives but renounced his connections with him once he realized that Blackstone was engaged in missionary work among the Jews.[47] In his reply to Felsenthal, Blackstone insisted that evangelization efforts and the attempt to spread the Gospel are an inherent part of the Christian creed.[48]

This exchange of letters reflects the misunderstanding over the issue of the mission between dispensationalists and Jews, and between Christians and Jews in general. Jews reject the attempts to evangelize them. They see in the Christian mission a threat to Jewish survival, for converted Jews were torn out of the Jewish nation. Moreover, they consider the mission an indication of the illegitimacy of Judaism from the Christian viewpoint and an expression of contempt, which indicates that Christians look on Jews as inferior, wretched people who need to be converted to the "right" religion.[49] The dispensationalists, however, saw in their efforts to evangelize Jews not a sign of contempt but a sign of good will and dedication.[50] Although dispensationalist missionaries were not always free from prejudices, they believed that they were true friends of the Jewish people and that the years they dedicated to the attempt to evangelize Jews were proof of this friendship. Donations to missions to the Jews were sometimes sent anonymously from "a friend of Israel."[51] The dispensationalist missionaries were aware that Jews tended sometimes to treat them with animosity but saw this as a sign of ungratefulness. They remained convinced that their work was an expression of good will.

The Christian-Jewish Conference, 1890

In 1888-1889, Blackstone visited Palestine. He described the barrenness and emptiness of the country in relation to the Jewish nation: "a land without a people and a people without a land."[52] Blackstone was impressed by the development the new Zionist immigration to Palestine since 1882 had brought about. The new Zionist settlements were a "sign of the times" that gave validity and encouragement to the dispensationalist hopes. They were a proof that one was witnessing the last stage of the current dispensation and that the great events were not only at hand, but had as a matter of fact actually started and that the coming of the Lord was to be expected very soon.[53] Since the 1880s, dispensationalists have taken a close look at the Zionist movement, the developments in the Jewish settlements in Palestine, and the birth of the state of Israel and have pointed to them as a fulfillment of biblical prophecies and a sign that the dispensationalist understanding of God's plans for humanity was correct.

The visit to Palestine probably encouraged Blackstone to take a more active line concerning the Jewish fate.[54] In November 1890, he organized a conference of Christians and Jews to discuss "the past, present and future of Israel." The conference was held at the First Methodist Episcopal Church in Chicago. The Jewish participants included three Reform rabbis: Emil G. Hirsch, Bernhard Felsenthal, and Joseph Stolz. The Christian (actually Protestant) participants included premillennialist figures as well as nonpremillennialists, including professors from theological seminaries in Chicago.[55]

The idea of a Jewish restoration to Zion was raised in the conference by the Rev. J. M. Caldwell, a Methodist minister and a dispensationalist, who spoke of "Jerusalem and Palestine as they are today, and the Restoration of Israel." "I can have no doubt about the restoration of Israel," he said. "Not only does the Bible declare it, but the signs of the times all indicate that the realization is near at hand."[56] Rabbi Emil G. Hirsch of Sinai congregation in Chicago, a noted spokesmen of the radical wing in Reform Judaism and the founder of the *Reform Advocate*, responded by expressing an opinion that was current in American Jewish Reform circles:

> We modern Jews do not wish to be restored to Palestine. We have given up hope in the coming of a political personal Messiah. We say, "the country wherein we live is our Palestine, and the city wherein we dwell is our Jerusalem." We will not go back . . . to form again a nationality of our own.[57]

Despite disagreement over the return of the Jews to the land of Israel, the members of the conference were united in their concern for the fate of the Jews in Russia, who were subject to severe legal restrictions as well as the threat of pogroms. The conference issued a resolution that expressed "a disapprobation of all discrimination against the Jews 'as such' " and declared "sincere sympathy and commiseration to the oppressed Jews of Russia and the Balkans, the victims of injustice and outrage." It addressed "the rulers and eminent statesmen of the vast Russian Empire" and pleaded

> with all its fair minded and noble citizens in the name of God and the name of the common brotherhood of man, to stay the hand of cruelty from this time-honored people, which have given them as well as us our Bible, our religion, and our knowledge of God. Resolved, that we call upon the rulers and statesmen of our own country to use their influence and good offices with the authorities of all lands, to accomplish this humane and righteous end.[58]

The Blackstone Memorial, 1891

Encouraged by the success of the conference in passing a resolution in favor of the Russian Jews, Blackstone took upon himself a more ambitious task—the presentation of a petition to the president of the United States in favor of the restoration of Palestine to the Jews.[59] The petition, which is known as the Blackstone Memorial, reads as follows:

> What shall be done for the Russian Jews? It is both unwise and useless to undertake to dictate to Russia concerning her internal affairs. The Jews have

lived as foreigners in her dominions for centuries, and she fully believes that they are a burden upon her resources and prejudicial to the welfare of her peasant population, and will not allow them to remain. She is determined that they must go. Hence, like the Sephardim of Spain, these Ashkenazim must emigrate. But where shall 2,000,000 of such poor people go? Europe is crowded and has no room for more peasant population. Shall they come to America? This will be a tremendous expense, and require years.

Why not give Palestine back to them again? According to God's distribution of nations it is their home, an inalienable possession from which they were expelled by force. Under their cultivation it was a remarkably fruitful land, sustaining millions of Israelites, who industriously tilled its hillsides and valleys. They were agriculturists and producers as well as a nation of great commercial importance—the center of civilization and religion.

Why shall not the powers which under the treaty of Berlin, in 1878, gave Bulgaria to the Bulgarians and Servia to the Servians now give Palestine back to the Jews? These provinces, as well as Roumania, Montenegro, and Greece, were wrested from the Turks and given to their natural owners. Does not Palestine as rightfully belong to the Jews? It is said that rains are increasing, and there are many evidences that the land is recovering its ancient fertility. If they could have autonomy in government the Jews of the world would rally to transport and establish their suffering brethren in their time-honored habitation. For over seventeen centuries they have patiently waited for such a privileged opportunity. They have not become agriculturists elsewhere because they believed they were mere sojourners in the various nations, and were yet to return to Palestine and till their own land. Whatever vested rights, by possession, may have accrued to Turkey can be easily compensated, possibly by the Jews assuming an equitable portion of the national debt.

We believe this is an appropriate time for all nations, and especially the Christian nations of Europe, to show kindness to Israel. A million of exiles, by their terrible suffering, are piteously appealing to our sympathy, justice, and humanity. Let us now restore to them the land of which they were so cruelly despoiled by our Roman ancestors.

To this end we respectfully petition His Excellency Benjamin Harrison, President of the United States, and the Honorable James G. Blaine, Secretary of State, to use their good offices and influence with the Governments of their Imperial Majesties—

Alexander III, Czar of Russia;
Victoria, Queen of Great Britain and Empress of India;
William II, Emperor of Germany;
Francis Joseph, Emperor of Austr-Hungary;
Abdul Hamid II, Sultan of Turkey;
His Royal Majesty, Humbert, King of Italy;
Her Royal Majesty Marie Christiana, Queen Regent of Spain;

and the Government of the Republic of France and with the Governments of Belgium, Holland, Denmark, Sweden, Portugal, Roumainia, Servia, Bulgaria, and Greece. To secure the holding at an early date, of an international conference to consider the condition of the Israelites and their claims to Palestine as their ancient home, and to promote, in all other just and proper ways, the alleviation of their suffering condition.

Blackstone personally got people to sign the petition in Chicago, New York, Boston, Baltimore, Washington, and Philadelphia. Had he tried in other cities, he might have raised more signatures than the 413 he did, though the list of signers is impressive. Blackstone was often assisted in the collecting of signatures by letters of introduction. Rabbi B. Felsenthal, for example, gave Blackstone letters of recommendation to fellow rabbis.[60]

As a consequence, Blackstone established contacts with Zionist activists in America. One of them was Adam Rosenberg, a New York attorney and president of Hoveve Zion and later Shave Zion in New York. These pre-Herzlian Zionist organizations, whose memberships did not exceed a few dozen persons, encouraged Jewish settlement in Palestine.[61] Rosenberg, too, saw in Blackstone a friend and helper for the cause of Jewish settlement in Palestine. Once Rosenberg asked Blackstone to apply to Secretary of State Walter Gresham to act on behalf of the interests of Shave Zion.[62]

Although Blackstone presented his memorial as an aftermath of the Christian-Jewish conference, its contents reveal a complete break with the resolutions of the conference. In the conference resolutions there was no mention of the idea that Palestine should be returned to the Jews, and the conference pleaded with the rulers of Russia to improve the treatment of their Jewish subjects. The memorial, on the other hand, concluded that there were no future and hope for the Jews in Russia and they must leave. It thus suggested the return of Palestine to the Jews as a solution to the problem of Russian Jewry. The reason might be that while the resolution was not Blackstone's own suggestion but that of the conference as a whole, the memorial was entirely his initiative. He could define it as he wished and thus proposed in it his own suggestion for solving the problem of the Russian Jews.

Blackstone was very careful not to criticize Russia in his memorial. When he presented the memorial to President Harrison, Blackstone explained this point as follows: "Believing that protests against Russia would make matters worse . . . this memorial . . . [does not] antagonize Russia but seeks peaceably to give Jews control of their home in Palestine."[63]

It seems that Blackstone found in the unfortunate situation of Russian Jewry an opportunity to promote the idea of the restoration of Palestine to the Jews. While he undoubtedly cared for the fate of the Jews around the world, Blackstone was motivated first and foremost by his premillennialist hopes. The state of the Jews in Russia concerned the American public.[64] The United States had intervened a few times on behalf of Jews in Russia. On August 20, 1890, the U.S. House of Representatives passed a resolution requesting the president to communicate to the House any information that he might possess concerning the persecution of Jews in Russia.[65]

Most of the people who signed the petition were not premillennialists. They were rather responding to Blackstone's humanitarian call. "A million of exiles, by their terrible suffering, are piteously appealing to our sympathy, justice, and humanity," wrote Blackstone in his memorial. He accompanied his call to give the Russian Jews Palestine with political, legal, and economic reasoning. On the political and legal levels, Blackstone pointed to precedents in the new national states that were created in Europe in the nineteenth century by means of international consent. If the Congress of Berlin (1878) could decide in favor of the establishment of an independent Bulgarian state in what was formerly a Turkish territory, the same could be done concerning a Jewish state in Palestine. For economic reasons, Blackstone argued, world Jewry could help finance both the settlement of "their suffering brethren in their time-honored habitation" and compensate Turkey for "whatever vested rights by possession" she had in Palestine.

Although Blackstone based his plan for the restoration of Palestine to the Jews on humanitarian, political, legal, and economic reasons, and although the premillennial hope does not appear in the petition, it nevertheless does reflect a strong religious-biblical reasoning. The Jewish claim to Palestine is based on "God's distribution of nations." Blackstone saw it as the duty of "the Christian nations of Europe to show kindness to Israel." The Christian-biblical appeal of the petition reflects, among other things, the impact of the Bible on Protestant America.

One cannot accept Peter Grose's suggestion that a major motivation for signing the petition was "the need to do something lest teeming crowds of immigrants would make life too uncomfortable for American society."[66] As Grose's own book proves, anti-Semitism almost never inspired support for Jewish national restoration in Palestine. As for the well-rooted Jews of German background, those among them who opposed the idea of a Jewish settlement in Palestine came out against the petition and what it represented.

Blackstone's proposal appeared five years before Theodore Herzl, the father of political Zionism, published *Der Judenstaat* and six years before Herzl convened the first Zionist congress in Basel. There is a striking resemblance between Blackstone's and Herzl's proposals for the establishment of a Jewish state in Palestine. The two men came forth publicly and solemnly with a plan for the transportation and settlement in Palestine of millions of Jews en bloc and the establishment of a Jewish state there. The two of them believed that this should and could be done by means of international consent, that Turkey could be convinced to give up Palestine and would be compensated by Jewish financial support to help her balance her deficit. The schemes of both men were based on a great amount of optimism. They thought that Turkey would consent, that the great political powers would give their hands to such a plan, and, most of all, that the Jews would emigrate en masse to Palestine should a Jewish national state be built there. Although the dispensationalist belief could be described as alienated from the idea of progress, one can find in Blackstone's scheme the deep influences of the liberal thinking of his age. In both Herzl's and Blackstone's suggestions is the basic assumption that problems—even cardinal and complex ones—can be solved by means of reason and persuasion, and that plans, even grandiose ones, can be carried out.

Blackstone, like Herzl after him, took little notice in his plans of the fact that there were non-Jewish inhabitants in Palestine. He had visited Palestine and considered it an empty and deserted land. He did not think that the small Arab population that lived in Palestine should be an obstacle to Jewish restoration.[67]

There are, however, some major differences between Blackstone's and Herzl's schemes. Herzl's aim was the security and well-being of the Jewish people. Blackstone's aim, or rather, hope, was the Second Coming of Jesus, which was to be preceded by the return of the Jews to their land. The settlement in Palestine and the establishment of a national state were not intended to secure the lives of the Jews. Years of great turmoil were waiting for them in the "time of Jacob's trouble." While Herzl's scheme was that of a Jew concerned with the fate of his brethren, Blackstone's approached the problem of the Jews' insecure life in certain parts of the world from an angle that was, for the most part, alien to the intrinsic needs of the Jews. Their fate was not an aim but a means in an eschatological scheme in which they were to play a central role. Although Blackstone's proposals preceded Herzl's by a few years, he had no direct influence on Herzl. Blackstone's memorial provoked much comment in America but was hardly known in Europe.[68]

The Blackstone Memorial provoked an unprecedented editorial debate in the American Jewish community.[69] The American Zionists welcomed Blackstone's initiatives. Wolf Schur, the editor of *Ha Pisga*, the only Hebrew periodical at that time in America, warmly endorsed the memorial. Although he was apprised of Blackstone's messianic motivations, he concluded:

> It is not their intention to bring us under the wings of Christianity in our time
> ... but rather in the days to come when peace returns and each of us sits under
> his fig tree and vine, and after the battle of Gog and Magog. Let the Christians
> do whatever they can to help us in the resettlement in Palestine. As to the
> question of our faith, let that rest until Elijah returns and then we shall see
> whether or not their dream materializes.[70]

Schur's reaction was based on the assumption that the dispensationalist hopes would never materialize. His attitude has remained up to this day the predominant Zionist attitude toward the dispensationalist support of the Zionist cause. Schur was not aware of all the details of the premillennialist eschatological scheme, which included the prospect of "the time of Jacob's trouble." He was equally unaware that it was indeed the intention of the premillennialists to bring Jewish people "under the wings of Christianity" at this time and age, and that the premillennialist hopes inspired not only support for Zionism but also vigorous missionary activities among the Jews.

The other Jewish periodicals that endorsed the Blackstone Memorial were *The American Hebrew* and *Menorah*, the official organ of B'nai B'rith, which favored the idea of the Jewish settlement in Palestine but opposed the idea of a Jewish state.

> To ask for any more than for a guarantee from the Sultan for the protection of
> colonists would be utopian, futile and needless. Any attempt to setting up a
> Jewish state would arouse the jealousies of the various Churches as well as the
> government. Such a move would not even meet the support of the wealthy and
> educated Jews over the world who have become as attached to the country of
> their birth and choice as any other citizen of the various commonwealths.[71]

It is evident that the editors of *Menorah* felt that support for the idea of a Jewish state might be interpreted as a sign of disloyalty to their own country.

Many Jewish organs reacted negatively to Blackstone's Memorial; many of the editors were concerned with their own fate as American Jews. The *Jewish Messenger* stated:

First, it revives the old reproach of the anti-Semites that the Jews cannot be patriots if Palestine is their national home today. Secondly, it makes the Jews again a subject of newspaper comment when such publicity and notoriety work more harm than good.

Curiously, the *Jewish Messenger* believed that "the Jewish problem will be solved in Russia and Russian enlightened opinion."[72]

The *American Israelite*, the leading Reform periodical in the United States, also rejected the plan. Its editors were afraid that the establishment of a Jewish state would induce countries in which the Jews "compete for prominence and have achieved success" to expel their Jews to Palestine.[73] Some other Jewish periodicals, such as the *Jewish Voice* and the *Reform Advocate*, Emil G. Hirsch's organ, rejected Blackstone's plan as well.[74]

Although the petition evoked much negative reaction in the Reform camp, seventeen Reform and Conservative rabbis signed the memorial. It is not surprising that Conservative rabbis like H. Pereira Mendes and Marcus Jastrow signed the petition. The Conservative movement in American Judaism had emerged as a reaction to what was considered a too radical break with Jewish traditions and law. But the fact that Reform rabbis—among them one outstanding leader in the Reform movement at the time, Kaufman Kohler, of Temple Beth-El in New York—signed the petition is astonishing and raises a serious question concerning the attitudes of the Reform movement toward the idea of the Jewish return to Palestine. Kohler himself was one of the initiators of the Pittsburgh Platform, a declaration of principles adopted by a meeting of Reform rabbis in 1885 that had become the accepted credo of the Reform movement. The Pittsburgh Platform advocated the complete absorption into Judaism of the principles of rationalism. It reflected a spirit that seems alien to the idea of Jewish national restoration. For instance:

> We recognize in the modern era of universal culture of heart and intellect the approach of the realization of Israel's great Messianic hope for the establishment of the kingdom of truth, justice, and peace among all men. We consider ourselves no longer a nation but a religious community, and therefore expect neither a return to Palestine . . . nor the restoration of any of the laws concerning the Jewish state.[75]

The memorial, on the other hand, implied that in Palestine, the Jews would create there a national state. Palestine was described as "their home, an unalienable possession from which they were expelled."

76

In truth, however, many Reform rabbis were ambivalent toward the idea of a Jewish restoration to Palestine. Kaufman Kohler provides a good example. Although he declared the Jews to be merely a religious community, Kohler referred to the Jews numerous times as a nation.[76] He called for unity and solidarity of Jews around the world and for the establishment of a Pan-Jewish Congress.[77] Kohler supported and even rejoiced at the new Jewish settlements that were being built in Palestine.[78] He believed that a cultural and spiritual center for world Jewry could be built there.[79] Yet when Theodore Herzl came forth with a plan for the establishment of a Jewish state in Palestine in the late 1890s, Kohler denounced the plan. He considered the Jews to be a priest-people with a mission of spreading universal values among the nations. The Reform rabbi objected, therefore, to Herzl's idea that all Jews, including those in enlightened countries, should emigrate to Palestine.[80] However, while he condemned political Zionism he continued to support the colonization of Palestine.

> It is political Zionism that I condemn. Remember that I do not speak . . . of the plan of a simple and gradual colonization of Palestine. . . . There is however another side of Zionism which we heartily endorse. . . . While the hope of a national resurrection worked as incentive and inspiration, the arid soil of Judea was made to blossom forth a new with wheat and wine . . . and who whether Orthodox or Reform, will find fault with a sentiment so sacred and so stimulating as this.[81]

It might be that as the memorial referred to the restoration of the Russian Jews to Palestine Kohler found no fault in the plan. The Jews in Russia were oppressed and could not fulfill their mission as a priest nation. Kohler differentiated between the role of the Jews in the enlightened West and those in countries in which they were oppressed. The latter, he asserted, could not afford to be cosmopolitan.[82] Like the editors of *Menorah*, he might have supported the petition even though he did not believe that it would bring about the actual establishment of a Jewish state.

Kohler's attitude was not unique. For example, I. M. Wise, another outstanding leader of the Reform movement, opposed the idea of a Jewish state yet supported the Jewish settlement in Palestine.[83] One might see therefore in the attitude of the rabbis who were willing to endorse Blackstone's proposal the seeds and early beginnings of a favorable attitude toward Zionism in the Reform camp. About a decade later, two Reform rabbis—Judah L. Magnes and Stephen Wise—held leading positions in the Zionist Federation that was organized in the United States in response to Herzl's activity. Their attitude, however, was exceptional among Reform rabbis and a few more decades had to pass until Zionism became accepted and even normative for Reform Judaism.

The Chicago rabbis (as well as other Jewish leaders in the city) signed the memorial under a special addendum that referred to Jewish noninvolvement in agriculture. Blackstone stated in his memorial: "They have not become agriculturalists elsewhere because they believed they were mere sojourners in the various nations, and were yet to return to Palestine and till their own land." The addendum on the other hand claimed that: "Several petitioners wish it stated that the Jews have not become agriculturalists because for centuries they were almost universally prohibited from owning and tilling land in the countries of their dispersion." The signers of the addendum obviously wanted to emphasize that the Jews were loyal citizens of their countries who never intended to withdraw from any activity because of Jewish national expectations.

This attitude would to some extent become normative for American Jewish Zionists: They have been supportive of the establishment of a Jewish state and have seen in it a national and cultural center for world Jewry and a refuge for Jews in countries where they were persecuted. However, they did not cease to consider themselves loyal citizens of the United States. When Felsenthal or Kohler signed the memorial that called for the restoration of Palestine to the Jews, they absolutely did not mean that they themselves intended to settle in Palestine. It was up to Jews from other, less fortunate, countries to settle there.

The United States did take some steps in response to the Blackstone Memorial. The opinion of the American ambassador in Constantinople was asked and his answer was that the Turkish government would not part peaceably with any of its territory. Selah Merrill, the American consul in Jerusalem who was against the idea of the Jewish restoration to Palestine wrote that "Turkey was not in the habit of giving away whole provinces for the asking."[84] On April 6, 1891, the American ambassador to Russia, Charles Smith, met with Nicolai de Giers, the Russian minister of foreign affairs, and discussed with him the possibility of an international conference "to consider the conditions of the Israelites and the question of restoring Palestine to the hands of this people as the asylum and the home of such of their race as might choose to go from other lands." De Giers answered that if the United States would suggest a conference, Russia would cooperate.[85] The United States, however, never took any steps to try to convene such a conference nor ever seriously intended to do so.

In his third annual message to Congress on December 9, 1891, President Harrison spoke at length on the fate of Russian Jewry. He did not refer to the Blackstone Memorial or to the idea of the restoration of Palestine to the Jews, nor did he suggest any initiative of the United States. His concern was that the United States should not be flooded by multitudes of refugees from Russia: "the sudden transfer of such a multitude under conditions that tend to strip them of their small accumulations is neither good for them nor for us."[86]

Efforts Following the Petition

Although Blackstone's memorial failed to influence American policy, he did not treat his petition as a failure and did not give up his hope that the United States would take action to restore Palestine to the Jews. Between 1891 and his departure for China in 1908, Blackstone continued to correspond with President Harrison and the secretaries of state, James Blaine and later Walter Gresham, reminding them of the petition and repeating his request that the United States take diplomatic initiatives.[87]

In October 1891, Blackstone published "May the United States Intercede for the Jews?" In it, he added arguments for American support of the return of Palestine to the Jews. He argued that such support would not be a violation of the Monroe Doctrine. Moreover, as the United States had no imperialistic aspirations in the Middle East, she was the most suitable country to initiate political changes in that area. The international powers would acknowledge that her motivations were unselfish. Being aware of opposition to giving the holy places of Christianity to the rule of Jews, he wrote: "possession of Christian holy places, can as well be arranged under Jewish as under Turkish rule. Indeed, so small a state . . . would of necessity realize the importance of justice, righteousness and moderation."[88]

In March 1893, Blackstone wrote to Secretary of State Walter Gresham and asked for an interview to discuss the issue of who would be appointed the new U.S. consul in Jerusalem.[89] The previous consul, Selah Merrill, had not been in favor of the Jewish settlement of Palestine.[90] Blackstone obviously wanted to see a consul who would be more favorable toward the Jewish population in Palestine and toward the new Zionist immigration.

Blackstone did not abandon his hope for an international conference of the world powers that would decide on the restoration of Palestine to the Jews. In his attempts to renew the interest in his 1891 petition, in 1894 Blackstone wrote to the Earl of Aberdeen, the governor general of Canada. He asked the governor's help to secure a favorable attitude of the British government to the idea expressed in his memorial. "Our government as you are aware is slow to take any action and especially the initiative in European affairs." However, if the British government would make "some unofficial expression of sentiment upon the subject" and the United States government would learn that its initiative on the matter would be successful, it might be moved to act.[91]

Blackstone also wrote to President Grover Cleveland. The United States was intervening at that time in favor of the Armenians in Turkey, and Blackstone took the opportunity to tell the president that, "The present agitation concerning the Armenians is in harmony with that concerning the Jews and their claims to Palestine that it is desired to revive the memorial which was presented to General Benjamin Harrison." He ended his letter by stating that "there has not been such an affortunate time to show kindness to Israel since the days of Cyrus King of Persia."[92]

In 1892, Blackstone had tried to summon a second Jewish-Christian conference, presumably to try to recreate a momentum for the idea of the Jewish restoration to Palestine in American public life.[93] However, this conference did not materialize.

On June 15, 1903, the Chicago Methodist Preachers Meeting endorsed Blackstone's memorial of 1891. The preachers' resolution was sent to President Theodore Roosevelt together with the original memorial of 1891. The resolution reads as follows:

> WHEREAS the civilized world seeks some feasible method of relieving the persecuted Jews, and
> WHEREAS we recognize the difficulty of harmonizing the widely divergent races of the multitudinous population of Russia and
> WHEREAS its government should properly resent any foreign interference with its internal affairs, and
> WHEREAS Russia can consistently point to Austria, Persia, Roumania, Morocco and the French possessions in North Africa as evidence that the Jews are not in her dominion alone, oppressed and slaughtered and
> WHEREAS the Jewish question is worldwide and demands an international remedy, and

WHEREAS the environment of the Jews is so fraught with alarming danger in many quarters of the world that humanity and the Golden Rule of Our Master demand speedy action, and

WHEREAS the Jews, when expelled from Spain, were given an asylum in Turkey and have, since then, received such comparatively kind treatment in the Sultan's Dominions as to give assurance that some satisfactory arrangement can now be made for their permanent re-settlement in Palestine, and

WHEREAS a Memorial was presented by Mr. Wm. E. Blackstone in 1891 to Hon. Benjamin Harrison then President of the United States entitled "What shall be done for the Russian Jews" in which it was prayed that the good offices of this government might be used to intercede with the governments of Europe for an international conference to consider the condition of the Jews and their right to a home in Palestine, and

WHEREAS the remarkable endorsement of the Memorial by eminent statesmen, clergymen, philanthropists, financiers, and the religious and secular press of our country, as well as our most prominent Jewish citizens, cannot fail to emphasize the wisdom of the plan proposed, and

WHEREAS we deem the present moment most opportune for calling such an International conference of the Powers,

NOW THEREFORE, be it resolved by the Methodist Ministers of Chicago, duly assembled on this fifteenth day of June, 1903, that we respectfully commend the Memorial aforesaid and the action therein prayed, to the earnest attention of our Government for such measures as may be deemed wise and best for the permanent relief of the Jews.

Resolved that a copy hereof, together with a copy of the Memorial, be immediately forwarded by our Secretary to the honorable Theodore Roosevelt, President of the United States, and to hon. John Hay, Secretary of State.[94]

According to Blackstone, the resolution of the Methodist Preachers Meeting was due to his initiative.[95] This is very likely true. The Methodist Preachers Meeting was the first among several Protestant bodies that adopted such a resolution on Blackstone's initiative. The resolutions that were issued by the other church bodies were almost identical to this one and it seems probable that Blackstone helped define its content. Blackstone was masterful in securing help and endorsement for his schemes from some of the mainline Protestant churches in America.

Blackstone continued to write and publish premillennial tracts and pamphlets, some of them concentrating on his understanding of the Jewish problem and on the idea of the Jewish restoration to Palestine. These pamphlets were often distributed as part of the missionary efforts among the Jews. The ideas that Blackstone expressed in these tracts were not different from those he had expressed in *Jesus is Coming*. His aim was to distribute shorter material on one theme.

In 1892, Blackstone published a small pamphlet entitled *Jerusalem*.[96] The pamphlet, which reflects Blackstone's impressions from his visit in Palestine, gives a brief history of the country, describes the Jewish settlement there and the new neighborhoods in Jerusalem, and presents an encouraging attitude concerning the future of Israel in that land.[97] The pamphlet does not describe the dark sides of the future of Israel in Blackstone's beliefs ("the time of Jacob's trouble"). It was the pamphlet most distributed by Blackstone to Jews.[98]

In *The Millennium*, a pamphlet published in 1904, Blackstone concentrated on convincing his readers of the validity of the pursuit of the millennium. Like other dispensationalists, he made a claim regarding the antiquity and universality of the belief in the millennium, and its reliance on both the Old and New Testaments. In this tract as in others Blackstone referred at length to the Jewish people and the Zionist movement, both of which were central to his millennial scheme.

The Heart of the Jewish Problem was distributed to Jews as part of the evangelization campaign of the mission. Blackstone's main message to the Jews in this pamphlet is that Jesus Christ is their one and only Savior and that only through belief in him can they fulfill themselves as Jews. The heart of the Jewish problem is not the issue of national survival but of the acceptance of Jesus.

The Arbitration Memorial

Blackstone's grandiose plans, including the initiative of memorials concerning international matters, were not limited to his Zionist hopes. In 1893, Blackstone carried out an outstanding enterprise of signing up notable people to a memorial propagating change on an international scale—this time concerning international arbitration. The initiative to organize this memorial was inspired by the World Columbian Exposition that took place in Chicago from May 1 until October 30, 1893. The exposition was authorized by the Congress of the United States to commemorate the four hundredth anniversary of the discovery of America by Christopher Columbus. It attracted more than 27,000,000 visitors. An interreligious congress, The World's

Parliament of Religions, was summoned as part of the events of the exposition.

Blackstone found in the Columbian Exposition an opportunity to carry out his appeal for a court of international arbitration. Blackstone managed to turn it into an official enterprise of the World's Columbian Exposition Commission rather than his own singular attempt. Blackstone was appointed honorary commissioner of the exposition with the task of "securing . . . the completion of the memorial and its presentation to the various governments of the world." The memorial suggested that the governments of the world "unitedly agree, by mutual treaties, to submit for settlement by arbitration all such international questions and differences as shall fail of satisfactory solution by peaceful negotiations."[99] Blackstone's idea was "the determination of international controversies by Tribunals of Arbitration, or better still, by the judgments of an International Court of Justice."[100] The memorial was signed by four hundred notable persons from over forty countries.[101] It was presented to the secretary of state to transmit "to the several Governments of the World." This memorial, like Blackstone's other grandiose plans, produced no immediate results.[102]

Blackstone's involvement in the Arbitration Memorial raises a question. How did Blackstone, the eminent premillennialist who believed in the imminent return of Christ, get involved in an initiative which, at least on the surface, seeks to reform humanity and solve one of its most distressing problems through human effort? Was Blackstone manifesting a reformist-postmillennial notion in his effort to bring the governments of the world to agree on an international court of justice that would settle disputes between nations? The Arbitration Memorial does represent a belief in progress and in the ability of people to reform the condition of humanity by rational decisions.

Blackstone, however, might have had another concern. He wanted to prepare the world for the arrival of his Lord Jesus Christ. Blackstone held the conviction that the nations would be judged by Jesus.[103] Their behavior prior to his arrival would determine their chances of being saved. This notion, which played a dominant role in Blackstone's understanding of the role the United States should play in international politics, affected his expectations from other nations as well.

In 1902, Blackstone warned Britain against her wrongdoing in the international sphere. He called for Britain to repent and atone before the wrath of God would reach her. Blackstone's main accusation against Britain was that she had committed atrocities in China and was involved in the opium trade there. Another complaint was that Britain had declared war on the Boers in South Africa without first letting the International Tribunal in the Hague pass judgment on their dispute. "Remember that Nations are judged in this life. Bend thy knee quickly. . . . The clouds of God's wrath are gathered upon thee."[104]

In a letter to the archbishop of Canterbury, written during World War I, a war that Blackstone considered to anticipate the end of days, Blackstone suggested that the British should offer to pay the Chinese people

> at least $1,000,000,000 as some compensation for the damage suffered by the poor, defenseless but multitudinous people. Believing most sincerely and with the most intense solicitude that the danger does exist, yea, that our God's uplifting hand of judgment is impending over the Empire, may I implore you to warn the whole British people, that neither dreadnaughts, nor armies can save the Empire, unless there be first a genuine confession of, and repentance for the unparalleled sin of the opium crime against China, and an effort to make atonement.

Blackstone was not as naive as he might seem. He knew perfectly well that England would not pay such a vast sum as reparations to the Chinese people. He nevertheless considered it his duty to warn England of the awaiting wrath of God, to ask her to repent, and to suggest a means of repentance. Blackstone knew that his campaign might be futile, but he considered it his duty to make the effort anyhow. "I believe He [Jesus] wishes me to send this message to You," he wrote the archbishop.[105]

In 1908, Blackstone's wife died and he decided to go to China and join his son who was working there as a missionary. Blackstone became engaged in missionary work himself. He did not know Chinese, so he concentrated on distributing literature, including dispensationalist tracts, throughout the Far East. On his return journey to America, in 1914, Blackstone went through the Persian Gulf, and while stopping in Baghdad, he distributed pamphlets among the Jews of that city.

In 1916 Blackstone was appointed trustee of the Milton Stewart Fund. Stewart, who was the president of Union Oil Company of California, entrusted Blackstone with a $2 million fund intended for evangelistic work throughout the world. Blackstone ran the fund, the value of which had increased by 1932 to $6 million, almost until the end of his life. He used the fund to finance missionary publications for Jews.[106] It was through the

Stewart Fund that he financed dispensationalist missionary activities among the Jews of Eastern Europe.[107]

While Blackstone was returning from China and taking upon himself the administration of an evangelistic fund, worldwide events were taking place, events that caused him to become engaged once again in activity on behalf of the return of Palestine to the Jews.

The 1916 Memorial

In 1916, Blackstone initiated the presentation of another memorial to the president of the United States concerning the restoration of the Jews to Zion. This memorial is to some extent more important than the one of 1891, since it might have had more effect. The 1916 memorial interwove with other efforts to persuade President Wilson to favor the ideal of a Jewish national home in Palestine and to support the Balfour Declaration of 1917. His activity in behalf of this memorial marks the peak of Blackstone's involvement with the Zionist movement.

The idea of renewing the appeal of 1891 to President Harrison came from Nathan Straus, the owner of R. H. Macy and an active Zionist, with whom Blackstone was in close connection.[108]

Although Blackstone was seventy-five years old in 1916, he was fully in control of his mind and senses. He nevertheless set out on a less ambitious task than he had in 1891. This time he collected only eighty-two signatures. The list of signers, as with the first petition, included editors of newspapers, bishops, and presidents of banks and financial associations. Blackstone limited his efforts to four cities: Los Angeles, Chicago, New York, and Ithaca, N.Y., in all of which he had had to spend time anyhow. He did not go out of his way to collect signatures. Apparently Blackstone was not concerned this time with how many signed the petition. The fact that the idea of the restoration of Palestine to the Jews received strong endorsement from the American public was proved, as far as he was concerned.[109] The 1916 petition is virtually identical to the Methodist preachers' resolution of 1903. It was officially endorsed by bodies of major Protestant denominations. On May 26, 1916, the General Assembly of the Presbyterian Church, U.S.A., adopted Blackstone's petition as its own resolution[110] and presented it to President Wilson. The Methodist Ministers' Meeting of Southern California endorsed Blackstone's petition on May 1, 1916. So did the Presbyterian Ministerial Association of

Los Angeles, on May 8, 1916, and the Los Angeles Baptist Ministers Conference, on May 15, 1916.[111]

Blackstone was in close contact with the leaders of these major Protestant denominations and their endorsements were to a large degree due to his persuasion. Blackstone used his connections and influence with leaders of mainline Protestant denominations to organize a formal committee for the presentation of the petition to President Wilson. The members of the committee were Bishop J. W. Bashford of the Methodist church; Dr. F. M. North, president of the Federal Council of Churches of Christ in America; Dr. Robert E. Speer, secretary of the Presbyterian Board of Foreign Missions; and Dr. John R. Mott, general secretary of the International Committee of YMCAs. When Blackstone realized that he himself might not be able to participate in the presentation of the memorial to the president, he authorized these church leaders to present it without him.[112]

Blackstone labored unsuccessfully to get the Federal Council of Churches of Christ in America to endorse the petition as well as to serve as an official committee for its presentation. The council was an organization in which many Protestant denominations in America participated, including ones that did not endorse Blackstone's petition: the Lutheran General Synod, the Disciples of Christ, and the Mennonite church. Blackstone's request, which was brought up by Dr. H. K. Carroll, secretary of the Washington office of the federation, in November of 1916, was turned down by the Advisory Council of the Federation.[113] Although many of the church leaders who supported Blackstone were not dispensationalists, it seems that his initiatives found a more approving audiences among members of denominations that were, in general, part of the Reform tradition as well as shaped by nineteenth-century American revivalism.

Blackstone's connections with the leaders of the mainline Protestant churches and his ability to bring them to support the idea of the restoration of Palestine to the Jews illustrates the difference between American Protestantism of World War I and today. Although the modernist-conservative debate had already emerged, the borderline between liberal and evangelical Protestantism was not yet fully defined. Blackstone had access to the heart of Protestant America and American culture in general. After the modernist-conservative debate had reached its dramatic climax in the mid-1920s with the Scopes trial, evangelical Protestantism was no longer at the center of American civilization, and it is doubtful if an evangelical activist could mobilize liberal denominations to act on behalf of his eschatological hopes.

Whereas in 1891 Blackstone had signed up notable persons to his petition and presented it to the president all on his own, in 1916 he worked in close connection with the leaders of the Zionist movement. In the twenty-five years that had passed between the first initiative and the second one, American Zionism had developed from an insignificant group of a few dozen members that had little effect on American Jewish public life into a movement that embraced several thousand and attracted the devotion of some of America's most prominent Jews. Among its members was Louis D. Brandeis. Brandeis was chairman of the Provisional Executive Committee for General Zionist Affairs[114] until July 21, 1916, when he became an associate justice of the Supreme Court. He continued to serve as the honorary president of the committee and was its actual leader.

The American Zionist leaders took interest in and responded favorably to Blackstone's pro-Zionist activity. Nathan Straus; Stephen Wise, a Reform rabbi from New York who became the chairman of the Provisional Executive Committee for General Zionist Affairs; Jacob De Hass, who served as the secretary of that committee, and Brandeis himself found Blackstone's work beneficial to the Zionist cause. The American Zionist leaders were engaged in 1916-1917 in efforts to make the American government support the establishment of a Jewish national home in Palestine and were interested in promoting Christian support of their cause. In their letters to Blackstone, written while he was in the process of enlisting support for his petition, Straus and Brandeis urged him to concentrate on Christian signatures.[115]

The American Zionist leaders were well aware of Blackstone's premillennial thinking. He sent them copies of his books and pamphlets, letters discussing his eschatological understanding of the role and fate of the Jewish people, and even premillennial material that was to be kept in a safe place and opened only after the rapture had taken place. His forecast that great turmoils were waiting for Israel after the rapture and that only a part of the Jewish people would survive the Great Tribulation was not kept secret. In a Zionist conference in Los Angeles in January 1918, Blackstone openly expressed his opinion that those Jews who would neither convert to Christianity nor immigrate to Palestine were doomed to perish.[116]

The Zionist leaders had followed in Schur's footsteps. As they did not believe in the dispensationalist eschatological scheme, they therefore considered Blackstone's help to the Zionist cause to be the only concrete expression of the American Protestant premillennial hope regarding the Jewish people and Palestine. Although they were aware of Blackstone's hopes that Jews would convert to Christianity, they might have been unaware of the scope of his actual involvement in missionary work. That premillennial hopes motivated a large portion of the missionary work done among Jews was a fact they could not know. These Jewish leaders were no experts on Christian missions to the Jews and could not tell one Protestant mission from another. In addition, although Jews were irritated by the attempts to evangelize them, they held to the still current myth that only very few Jews converted to Christianity because of missionary work. Jews have developed a cynical attitude toward Jewish conversion to Christianity. Their theory has been that conversions occur out of socioeconomic motivations and not out of inner conviction, and that religious persuasion has little to do with it.[117]

The Zionist leaders treated Blackstone as an honored friend. He was invited to participate in Zionist conferences.[118] Some Zionists, like Nathan Straus, corresponded periodically with him, congratulating him on holidays and expressing their concern when he did not feel well. The relationship between Blackstone and this group of leaders was one of mutual trust. Stephen Wise, for example, shared with him his bitterness toward his foe, Judah Magnes.[119] Blackstone was entrusted with discreet duties as well.[120] Blackstone, for his part, entrusted Brandeis with carrying out his will, and in it he left his estate to the Zionist movement.[121] Blackstone also donated $5,000 to the Emergency Fund that was organized by the Provisional Executive Committee for General Zionist Affairs to help Jewish refugees and victims of the war in Eastern Europe and Palestine.[122] Blackstone's gesture was almost unique among American dispensationalists, who as a rule did not contribute money to Zionist efforts.

Blackstone was ready to present his memorial to the president, or rather let the committee of church leaders do that, in November 1916,[123] but the Zionist leadership kept him from doing so, claiming that the time was not ripe and that it should be presented to Wilson when he could pay it full attention.[124]

President Wilson not only knew about the memorial but also saw it "unofficially" a few times. Blackstone sent him a copy of it for "consideration." Wise had shown it to him twice.[125] Wilson also received a copy of the petition with the endorsement of the three conferences of ministers in California and the General Assembly of the Presbyterian Church, U.S.A. A formal solemn presentation of the petition, however, kept being delayed, and never actually took place.[126] Blackstone was willing to leave the decision as to the public presentation of the memorial to the Zionist leadership, claiming that he had "no personal ambition nor desires in reference to the Memorial" and that his only concern was that "it may accomplish the best results for the Jewish people in all the world."[127]

It seems that Wilson was hesitant to accept Blackstone's petition publicly,[128] but did treat it seriously. He suggested changes that he thought should be made in it.[129] If he had considered it an unimportant, singular document, he could easily have given his consent to its presentation. The president of the United States was used to accepting petitions on various matters, including many he cared little for. Harrison had accepted Blackstone's petition solemnly, although he had no intention of carrying out its suggestions. One should note that the United States was not in a state of war with Turkey and an official, ceremonious acceptance of a public demand to take away a territory that was part of the Turkish Empire might not have been desirable to Wilson.[130] It was probably at that time (1916-1917) that Wilson had developed a favorable attitude toward the ideal of a Jewish national home in Palestine but he did not come out publicly in favor of Zionism until September 1918. His pro-Zionist sentiments were kept hidden from his secretary of state, Robert H. Lansing, and from the State Department at large (and the American public), who knew nothing about the attitude Wilson had developed toward Zionism or anything about his consent to the issuing of the Balfour Declaration, which was also given behind their back.[131] It might be that his hesitation to accept the petition publicly was due to his unwillingness to expose his feelings concerning the return of the Jews to their land before he felt it was necessary to do so.

Although the petition was never formally presented, it did attain its goal. The petition was intended, as far as the Zionist leadership was concerned, to show the president that Protestant Christian America favored the idea of the Jewish restoration to Palestine. Together with the endorsement of the Presbyterian Church, U.S.A. and the meetings of ministers in California, it helped give the impression that this was the case. By the summer of 1917 the Zionist leaders were convinced of Wilson's support of their cause and saw no need to embarrass the president by presenting the petition to him publicly.[132]

What effect the petition had on Wilson is almost impossible to determine. Wilson left no clue as to what part Blackstone's petition and the churches' endorsement played in his conversion to the Zionist cause or in his approval of the Balfour Declaration and support of the establishment of a Jewish national home in Palestine under a British mandate in the peace talks in Paris in 1918-1919 (and in the San Remo Conference in 1920). Historians who have written about Wilson's role in the issuing of the Balfour Declaration have not even been aware of Blackstone's petition.[133]

Wilson was not a premillennialist,[134] and the eschatological reasoning Blackstone expressed in his private dispatches might not have impressed him. Wilson was, however, a committed Protestant. The son of a Presbyterian minister, he grew up in an evangelical atmosphere. Daily Bible reading was part of his routine. The Presbyterian church, which endorsed Blackstone's proposal, was his own church. Wilson revealed his Christian feelings concerning the Jewish home in Palestine twice, though not in public. In a private talk with Rabbi Stephen Wise in June 1917 he said: "To think that I, the son of a manse, should be able to restore the Holy Land to its people."[135] In February 1920, when the issue of the borders of Palestine was discussed in Paris, Brandeis wrote Wilson that it would be a betrayal of the promise of "Christendom" [for a national Jewish home in Palestine] if a decision was reached in favor of shrunken borders for Palestine. Wilson was moved and ordered Secretary of State Lansing to direct the American representatives in Paris to do their utmost to fulfill Brandeis's request.[136] However, whatever part religious sentiments played in shaping Wilson's favorable attitude toward Zionism, he was careful not to reveal them in public. If Wilson was impressed by Blackstone's petition and by the endorsement it received from Protestant bodies, including his own church, he would not have indicated that openly.

Voices in favor of a national Jewish home in Palestine were not the only ones expressed in the Protestant American arena. A pro-Arab Protestant lobby was organized in 1919 and was active at the Peace Conference in Paris. It consisted of missionaries associated with the Syrian Protestant College in Beirut (today the American University of Beirut), who were committed to Arab nationalism and favored the idea of an Arab state in "Greater Syria," which included Palestine.[137] In their view, the idea of a Jewish home in Palestine posed a threat to Arab national hopes and to their own interests in the Middle East as well. The pro-Arab Protestant group was one of the strongest and most energetic groups lobbying in Paris on behalf of the future of Palestine. One of its influential members was Cleveland H. Dodge, a close associate of Wilson.[138]

Blackstone took no steps to try to create a lobby to counterbalance the pro-Arab one. He continued to write to Wilson and share his opinions with him, but saw the establishment of a Jewish home in Palestine as a fait accompli.[139] In addition, Blackstone's tactics in carrying on his pro-Zionist activity had never included an attempt to establish a lobby. Although many in the dispensationalist camp were enthusiastic about the development of the Zionist movement and approved of Blackstone's pro-Zionist activity, no pro-Zionist organization emerged in the dispensationalist camp. Blackstone acted on his own.

One might see in the difference between the attitudes of Blackstone and the missionaries associated with the Syrian College the seeds of a division in American Protestantism in its attitude toward Zionism. While premillennialists have supported only the Zionist cause, the attitudes of American mainline liberal Protestants toward the Jewish restoration to Palestine are more varied and complex. Many sentiments, interests, and points of view played a part in shaping their attitudes.

Blackstone's Attitude Toward Zionism

Although Blackstone was a confirmed supporter of the Zionist cause, and in 1916-1917 worked closely with the Zionist leadership in America, his theoretical approach toward the movement was ambivalent. On the one hand, he rejoiced over the activity of the Zionist movement and the Jewish resettlement in Palestine. They were "signs of the time" that indicated the imminent coming of Christ and a proof that the end was at hand. Blackstone referred to these signs time and again.[140]

It seems that Blackstone had received from Zionism much more encouragement and help than he had given to it. The Zionist achievements gave validity to his messianic beliefs. After the Balfour Declaration was issued in November 1917, Blackstone, who received enormous encouragement from it, became so convinced that the coming of Jesus was soon to occur that he risked predicting a date by which the rapture would take place,[141] something that dispensationalists have usually avoided doing.[142]

The Jewish Era, the magazine that Blackstone edited for a while and to which he contributed hundreds of articles and letters over the years, published in each issue information concerning developments in the Zionist movement and the Jewish settlements in Palestine, always in a sympathetic tone.

But Blackstone perceived Zionism as no more than a tool, a means, for the fulfillment of the divine plan for the end of days. When discussing the movement's achievements, he was careful to note that it was by no means the fulfillment of God's plan for humanity. It was only a step in the process of the advancement of the ages. The Zionist movement, Blackstone observed, was a secular movement, which did not understand itself as a realization of biblical prophecies but rather sought to find a home and refuge for the Jewish nation.[143] This, however, it could not really achieve. A home and refuge for the Jewish people, Blackstone insisted, could be established only when they would accept Jesus Christ as their Savior.[144] The Jewish problem was not a secular one of refuge and survival, but a religious issue of recognizing their Messiah.

At one time, Blackstone protested against the secular character of Zionism. When he heard of Herzl's plan to "buy" the Turkish consent for giving up Palestine (though Blackstone himself had come up with almost the same suggestion in 1891), he sent Herzl a copy of the Bible in which he carefully marked down all the passages in which God had promised the land of Canaan to Israel.[145] Blackstone wanted to demonstrate his opinion that the land of Israel belongs rightfully to the Jews, as it was given to them by God and need not be bought. But behind that act stood his criticism of the Zionist movement.

The Role of the United States in Blackstone's Eschatological Understanding

The United States occupied a special role in Blackstone's understanding of the events that would take place at the end of days. He believed that the United States might be exempt from God's wrath and from the destruction that awaited other nations. He based his belief partly on his understanding of the United States as a God-fearing nation, which acts and behaves better than other nations.

Before the United States joined World War I, Blackstone considered it significant that the United States had kept out of the bloody and destructive war.[146] One of the major positive deeds of the United States, by which it had helped secure its salvation, was its treatment of its Jewish citizens.

Is it not possible that the United States, which has the wonderful acknowledgement of God stamped on its coinage "In God we trust" and whose national hymn ends with "Great God our king" and which has its annual Day of Thanksgiving for God's mercies and kindness and which has never persecuted Israel, is to be an exception to the general destruction which may be visited upon by the nations? Also that the wonderful promise of God to Abraham and his seed "I will bless them that bless thee, and curse them that curse thee" which has proved true in the history of the nations since the days of Nebuchadnezzar and even earlier, will be fulfilled in blessing to our country, which has been an asylum for the Jews from the persecuting nations of the world?[147]

The United States, Blackstone believed, was to take an active part in the restoration of Israel to its land and thus participate in preparing the ground for the Second Coming of Christ. Blackstone saw it as a mission that the United States had been assigned and should carry out.

No nation, in all past history, at all fits the prophecy, unless it be our own United States, which God has so wonderfully raised up, just before the harvest.
If our country is the prophecy's "Land shaddowing with Wings" [Isaiah 18], then the seventh verse indicates that we shall be specially used in the coming restoration of Israel to their God-given home in Palestine.[148]

The idea of the role assigned to America in restoring Israel to Zion was Blackstone's original innovation and contribution to the premillennial hope. He had developed that belief gradually and it had assumed its final shape by World War I, which Blackstone considered the beginning of the end of this age.[149]

Blackstone saw himself as a good American. He incorporated his sense of patriotism into his premillennialism by assigning to the United States a distinct role in his eschatological scheme. American dispensationalists have seen themselves as patriots. They have never considered their expectation of the Second Coming of Christ, which would mean the end of this age, to stand in contradiction to their loyalty to America. This marks a great difference between dispensationalists who take part in the American polity and such counterculture groups as Jehovah's Witnesses who also expect the arrival of Jesus and the establishment of his kingdom on earth, but reject the American state.

Conclusion

When World War I ended, Blackstone was in his late seventies. The petition of 1916-17 had been his last grand-scale public initiative. Living in Los Angeles, where he continued to run the Milton Stewart Fund, Blackstone continued to write letters to presidents Wilson and later Harding expressing his opinions on international political matters. He continued to take an interest in developments within the Zionist movement and subscribed to Zionist publications. Although Blackstone's name continued to appear as holding a responsible position in the Chicago Hebrew Mission, his actual connection with the mission was limited to letters he wrote to the mission that were published in the *Jewish Era*. He died in 1935 at the age of ninety-four.

William Blackstone's activity on behalf of the establishment of a Jewish commonwealth in Palestine was an outstanding phenomenon among early American dispensationalists. Although dispensationalists favored the idea of the return of the Jews to their land, they usually gave only passive support to the Zionist cause. The actual dispensationalist involvement with Jewish people and attempts to influence their destiny were concentrated in the realm of missionary work, a field in which Blackstone played a leading role.

Blackstone's pro-Zionist efforts were concentrated mainly on his attempts to bring the United States government to assume a leading role in securing international consent for the restoration of Palestine to the Jews, a role that he believed to have been assigned to the United States by God. His efforts in this realm were sporadic. He did not try to establish a permanent Protestant body for the advancement of the Zionist cause. With the exception of Woodrow Wilson, American presidents when making their decisions did not have to take into consideration that an important segment of American evangelical Protestantism favored the idea of the restoration of Palestine to the Jews. Such a situation came into being only in the 1970s.

Blackstone sincerely considered himself a friend of the Jews. He went out of his way more than once to help Jewish causes. In his interaction with Jews he showed friendliness and kindness. His activity in favor of the restoration of Palestine to the Jews was beneficial to the Zionist cause. Blackstone's motivations for promoting Zionism were, however, primarily his premillennial convictions and it is from that perspective that he saw the Jewish problem and the ways to solve it. Blackstone's treatment of the Jewish people was basically a means to an end—they were the people who would help bring about the Second Coming. His scheme for the future of the Jewish nation while the Great Tribulation takes place, for example, is far from being beneficial to the Jews. The Jews, according to this scheme, would have avoided the persecutions they had previously suffered in the Diaspora only in order to undergo no less severe turmoils at home.

By the same token, Blackstone saw Zionism as an instrument for setting Jews in Palestine and preparing the ground for the great events that would take place there after the rapture of the church. He regarded Judaism as a vehicle that kept the Jews waiting for the Messiah and for their return to their land. Blackstone had no patience with groups of Jews who had abandoned those hopes. He did not recognize any intrinsic value in Judaism, the religious and cultural heritage of the Jews, nor did he grant it legitimacy as a belief system that stands on its own.

One might conclude that Blackstone went out of his way to help the Jewish people for the sake of values and hopes that were for the most part foreign to them and to their long-range needs. The physical and cultural survival of the Jews was not his aim.

The evaluation of Blackstone's motivation raises a question concerning the usage and meaning of the term "Christian Zionism," which historians have often used in order to describe Christians who have supported the restoration of the Jewish people to Palestine.[150] Can the term "Zionist" refer to persons whose purposes are sometimes something other than the well-being of the Jewish people themselves? Ehle answers the question in the affirmative. He adopts a political definition of Zionism and considers Christians who worked toward the building of a Jewish home in Palestine as Zionists.[151] Franz Kobler, on the other hand, claims that "by virtue both of its origin and meaning (implying self-emancipation, religious and national renaissance) ['Zionist'] logically applies only to Jewish adherents of the movement."[152]

Zionism has incorporated into its midst a variety of groups and trends that expressed different opinions concerning the meaning of the Jewish national restoration. Some groups might not have agreed, therefore, with Kobler's definition of Zionism, and Ehle might be right in pointing to the political definition of Zionism, since it might have been the only goal on which all Zionists agreed. There is, however, one additional characteristic common to all Zionist trends. They have sought the well-being of the Jews as individuals and as a people. All Zionists have looked at the Jewish problem of physical and national survival from within, as people concerned about their own future. This cannot be said of those Christians who see in the Jewish restoration to Zion a means to an end, supporting it on account of hopes and values that have nothing to do with the well-being of the Jews or their needs. There is probably no use trying to change or replace the term "Christian Zionism," as it has been accepted and used in historiography. One needs, however, to bear in mind that the term stands for a different phenomenon from that generally denoted by the term "Zionism."

To a large extent Blackstone's pro-Zionist initiatives faded into obscurity. Historians of the Zionist movement usually were not even aware of his attempts and contributions. A temporary revival of interest in Blackstone took place in 1966. On the occasion of Israel's eighteenth anniversary and the seventy-fifth anniversary of the Blackstone Memorial, the American-Israel Society in the United States organized memorial meetings for Blackstone. Trees were planted in Israel in his memory at that time.

FIVE

Arno C. Gaebelein: Fundamentalist Leader and Missionary to the Jews

The Emergence of a Missionary to the Jews

Arno C. Gaebelein was born in 1861, in a village in Thuringia, Germany. Little is known about his childhood; Gaebelein starts his autobiography by recounting his experiences after he arrived in the United States in 1879.[1] He left his native country, Gaebelein writes, for various reasons; one of them was to escape compulsory military service.[2] After his arrival in America, he worked for a few months in a wool mill in Lawrence, Massachusetts.

Gaebelein had undergone a religious experience when he was twelve years old and accepted Jesus as his Savior. In Lawrence the new immigrant underwent a second religious experience. This time he decided to dedicate his life to the service of God. Gaebelein, who was previously a Lutheran, joined the Methodist Episcopal church. He started his service in this church as a Sunday school teacher, was licensed as an exhorter, and later on as a local preacher.

In 1881 Gaebelein moved to New York where he worked as an assistant to the minister of the German-speaking Methodist congregation on Second Street. In 1882 he became minister of a congregation in Baltimore, a position he held for three years. He was then appointed minister of a Methodist congregation in Harlem, New York, and later, in 1886, in Hoboken, New Jersey.

While working as a Methodist preacher in the New York area, Gaebelein was invited to preach in German before a Jewish audience in a mission to the

Jews headed by Jacob Freshman, himself a Jewish convert to Christianity. He preached there once a week for about a year. His involvement with Freshman's mission aroused his interest in the field of mission to the Jews. When his term as a minister in Hoboken had terminated in 1887, he asked permission of his bishop to work as a missionary among the Jews.

Gaebelein's first encounter with the premillennial belief had occurred early in the 1880s, when he read *Le Destin d'Israel* by Emil Guers, a French Huguenot pastor. It was not, however, until he began preaching the Christian belief to Jews that he became interested in the belief in the imminent Second Coming of Jesus, and was gradually convinced of it. Premillennialism gave more meaning to his evangelistic work. He was working to save some of God's chosen people, who were to play a central role in the divine plan for humanity. The premillennialist belief also made Gaebelein's missionary work more effective, for the idea of the return of the Jews to their land and the reestablishment of the kingdom of David had an appeal to Orthodox Jews. It correlated with some of their beliefs and hopes. The messianic hope of the premillennial belief was thus a tool for the missionary attempt to bring Jews to accept Jesus as their Savior.[3]

By the late 1880s, the Protestant missions to the Jews in America were mostly dispensationalist in their character. Recognizing the usefulness of the messianic approach, denominations and individuals who were not necessarily premillennialists often participated in sponsoring these enterprises.

Gaebelein acquired an outstanding knowledge of Judaism, which provided him with excellent tools to carry out his missionary work to the Jews. He did not graduate from a university or a theological seminary. His higher education consisted of only one year at Johns Hopkins University while he worked as a minister in Baltimore. The scope of his knowledge and the quality of his intellectual abilities were, however, like those of an academic scholar. Gaebelein was for the most part self-educated. He studied Semitic languages by himself and acquired a good knowledge of Hebrew. As he became interested in the Jewish heritage and in current trends in the Jewish culture, he became acquainted with both the rabbinical literature and the Hebrew literature of his days. He learned Yiddish, was able to speak it fluently, and wrote missionary tracts in that language. His knowledge of Yiddish and his acquaintance with Jewish customs and rites were such that Jews sometimes mistook him for one of their own.[4]

The Hope of Israel Mission

Gaebelein called the mission he established The Hope of Israel. The name manifested the idea the mission promoted, namely that Jesus was the only hope of the Jewish people. It was only through him that the Jewish people would be redeemed and would fulfill their religious and national hopes. The name further suggested the conviction that Israel had a hope and a future as a people.

The Hope of Israel mission was located in Rivington Street, on the Lower East Side, a section of New York that was inhabited in those years by tens of thousands of newly arrived Jewish immigrants from Eastern Europe. Gaebelein preached to Jewish audiences on Saturdays and on Jewish holidays. On the holidays, Gaebelein preached on themes related to the Jewish feasts and read prayers from the Jewish prayer book. His aim was to let the Jewish audience feel that they were not neglecting to celebrate their holidays by coming to hear his sermons. It also helped create an atmosphere that aimed at amalgamating Jewish customs with the Gospel. In his preaching, when he considered it not to stand in contradiction to the Gospel, he used rabbinical biblical hermeneutics as well as other rabbinical literature.

Gaebelein's preaching initially attracted an audience of about 250-300 people each Saturday, later on reaching a peak of over 500 listeners.[5] He preached twice, in the morning and in the afternoon. Although Jews have often looked unfavorably on missionary attempts to evangelize them, there obviously was no excommunication of Jews who participated as listeners in the mission's services and sermons or who accepted relief help from the mission. It seems that many of the young Jews who had recently arrived were curious to hear the Christian message. They did not necessarily consider the idea of conversion, but the sermons offered them a window to a culture and belief that were, on the whole, strange to them. The audience was, thus, not a stable one. Most people came a few times and after satisfying their curiosity and hearing what the preacher had to say, ceased coming.

In a few instances at the beginning of Gaebelein's weekly preaching some of his audience would protest against the Christian message; arguments and even stormy scenes would take place.[6] Gaebelein writes that when his Jewish audience found out that he was a Gentile his preaching was usually accepted much more tolerantly.[7]

In a few dramatic cases young Jews were convinced of Jesus' messiahship by what they heard in the Saturday morning sermons and declared their conversion there and then. But most often the decision to convert was a result of a long and painful inner struggle. Many people who contemplated the idea never made it to the actual act of conversion. Only a relatively small number of the many Jews who came in contact with the mission underwent conversion to Christianity.

Jewish historians tend therefore to evaluate the results of the missionary attempt on behalf of Protestants to evangelize the Jews in the nineteenth century, attempts that were often motivated by the messianic, premillennial hope, as a failure in comparison to the amount of work and hope that the missionaries had invested in it.[8] The Protestant missions managed to evangelize almost an insignificant percentage of the total Jewish population. The majority of the Jewish people were not impressed by the missionary message. This evaluation, although on the whole truthful, disregards some elementary features concerning Protestant premillennialist missionary enterprises.

The dispensationalist missionary attempt was not aimed at converting the whole of the Jewish nation. It was based on the realistic assumption that only a small part of the Jewish people would accept Christ in this age. Dispensationalists were motivated in part by the desire to save some of the Jewish people from the turmoil that was awaiting them in "the time of Jacob's trouble," which would occur at the time of the Great Tribulation, the seven years that were to separate the rapture of the church and the descent of Jesus and his saints to earth. Jews who accepted Jesus as their Lord and Savior were conceived by the majority of missionaries to have joined the body of the true Christian believers and be saved with them.[9] Jews who died without accepting Jesus as their Savior were believed to be doomed for eternity. On the other hand, those who would accept him and would die before the rapture of the church were to rise from the dead and join Christ in the air.

In addition to this consideration, which encouraged missionary zeal, dispensationalist missionaries acted on another major assumption connected with the their eschatological hope. As mentioned, according to the dispensationalist eschatological scheme 144,000 Jews would accept Jesus Christ as their Lord and Savior at the beginning of the Great Tribulation. These Jews would be persecuted by their own brethren, and some of them would be martyred. However, at the end of the Great Tribulation, the remnant of the Jewish people who would survive would accept Jesus as their Lord. They would be inspired by those Jews who had embraced Christianity at the beginning of the events. These 144,000 Jews would recognize the events as correlating with the Christian premillennial teachings they had learned while being exposed to dispensationalist missionary preaching and writing. They would be agents for spreading the Gospel and the truth of the messiahship of Jesus. The aim of the dispensationalist missions to the Jews was thus not merely to convert Jews at this time and age, but to spread the knowledge and truth of the Gospel among them. It was necessary that there should be 144,000 Jewish persons who would possess the knowledge of the Gospel (though they have not accepted it), so that they could fulfill their role whenever the rapture might come and the Great Tribulation begin.

One can often find in the accounts of dispensationalist missionaries to the Jews satisfaction and rejoicing over the mere existence and functioning of a missionary enterprise. For the dispensationalists, spreading the Gospel among the Jews was thus an aim in itself, regardless of how many people were converted.

In addition, most converts were in their twenties, the most promising period of their lives. They were usually dynamic, energetic, and ambitious. Their conversion filled the missionaries with deep satisfaction.

Although many missionaries did not convert more than a few dozen Jews, they were well pleased with the results of their efforts. Gaebelein, for example, looked back on his years as a missionary with pride. For him, as for other missionaries whose missionary endeavor was connected with messianic beliefs, it was a success.

One of the ways the Hope of Israel mission approached Jews was through relief and charitable work. The idea behind that work, which characterizes many Christian missionary enterprises, was that many Jews who would otherwise not be interested in listening to a missionary preaching the Gospel and who, in many cases, responded negatively toward attempts to evangelize them, would approach the mission out of need. Then, impressed by the good intentions and good will that were shown them, as well as thankful for the help they had received, they would develop a more favorable attitude toward the missionaries. They would tend more easily to open their minds and hearts to the truth of the Gospel.

The mission's activity was aimed at the newly arrived Jewish immigrants, many of whom were in need of material help. An impressive philanthropic work intended to help the poor Jews was carried out by upper-class German Jews. However, there was room for more help. The mission maintained a dispensary in which Jews could receive medical help free of charge or for a minimal fee. In the summer, it sponsored a summer camp for Jewish children. At Passover, it distributed matzos to poor Jews. Relief work as part of the missionary endeavor was not a novelty. The Chicago Hebrew Mission, for example, also sponsored similar enterprises. The distribution of matzos, on the other hand, was an innovation characteristic of Gaebelein's (and Stroeter's) attitude toward Jewish customs. It was a sign of respect toward a Jewish rite and served to signify that the Jewish customs were not an obstacle for the acceptance of Christ or a contradiction to participation in his body, the church.[10]

Christian missions were often criticized for attempting to bring the Jews to Christ by offering them economic benefits as well as a means to raise their social status and join America's Gentile middle class.[11] Gaebelein was indeed often approached by young Jews who inquired what benefits he could offer them if they converted. Would the mission, for example, finance their higher education and help them become doctors or lawyers? Gaebelein was not willing to offer extensive economic benefits in return for conversion.[12] He was interested not in "bought" converts, but in sincere ones who were convinced of the truth of the Gospel. Gaebelein criticized fellow missionaries who were offering financial benefits to converts or were using what he considered illegitimate methods in their attempts to approach Jews.[13] According to him, the missionaries who were using such techniques were mostly Jewish converts themselves,[14] an evaluation that correlates with that of Eichhorn.[15] Some of the conversions they made, Gaebelein claimed, were "a disgrace to both Judaism and Christianity."[16]

Gaebelein was not alone in his criticism of the financial benefits that were being offered to converted Jews. The question involved was, where does help for the needy end and a prize for the converted begin?[17] Criticism of missionaries who exercised unfair or untruthful propaganda in their enterprises was voiced at conferences, as was criticism against missionaries with dubious reputations. Gaebelein was stern and consistent in this respect.

David Eichhorn narrates elaborately the biographies of some converted Jews who directed missions to the Jews in America in the 1880s and 1890s and were, for the most part, dispensationalists. He portrays them as swindlers. Eichhorn's shortcoming is that he gives the impression that missions to the Jews in America were characterized by deceit on both sides. This, no doubt, was sometimes the case, but not the rule. One cannot accept Eichhorn's theory, which gives no credit to any sincere religious motivation that may have led some Jews to convert to Christianity and assumes that they were motivated merely by the prospect of social and economic convenience.[18]

Gaebelein's attitude toward Jewish converts to Christianity was one of appreciation and affection. He was not devoid of prejudices against Jews. But those among the Jews who opened their hearts and minds to the truth of the Gospel were the best in the lot.

Ernest F. Stroeter and the Hope of Israel Movement

The Hope of Israel mission reached the peak of its activity and turned into a major innovative enterprise in the years 1893-1899, when Dr. Ernest F. Stroeter joined Gaebelein in directing the mission.

Stroeter, like Gaebelein, was born in Germany and was a Methodist. Prior to his work in the Hope of Israel mission, Stroeter served as a professor at Denver University. An active premillennialist long before he joined Gaebelein, he participated in the International Prophetic Conference in Chicago in 1886. In his address, entitled "Christ's Second Coming—Premillennial," Stroeter broadly expressed his view of the role of the Jewish nation in the course of history and in the events that are to come. Stroeter's attitudes toward the Jewish people as expressed in his speech can be described as normative for dispensationalists. The Jews, he said, rejected their Messiah, Jesus, when he appeared for the first time. The misery that had befallen them since then resulted from that mistake.

> . . . the only people that had the Lord Jehovah for their political ruler have rejected Him, His statutes, His servants, yea, His only Son and are now become the byword of the nations, and their holy city, the city of the Great King (Matt. V., 35) is to this day trodden down by the Gentiles (Luke XXI., 24). God, indeed, did undertake the establishment of a perfect government in the earth. Man, His chosen people, caused the attempt to fail.

God, however, had not abandoned his promise to Israel, and a glorious future is awaiting them after the Second Coming of Jesus:

> Has God given up the plan forever? No: his gifts and calling, even to Israel are declared to be, by the apostle to the Gentiles, without repentance (Rom. XI, 29). . . . Israel must and is preserved to be chief among the nations (Jer. XXXI, 7). Out of Zion shall go forth the law and the word of the Lord from Jerusalem (Isa. ii, 3).[19]

Stroeter further emphasized in his speech the dispensationalist understanding of the Jewish people as the object of biblical prophecies and criticized the Christian biblical hermeneutical tradition that interpreted the nation and the land of Israel in spiritual terms.[20]

Gaebelein and Stroeter developed an attitude that was, to a large extent, innovative. They declared it to be the principle of the mission that Jews who accept Jesus as their Lord and Savior do not have to "Gentilize." They do not have to turn their backs on their Jewish heritage or cut their ties with the Jewish community. They were permitted to keep observing Jewish rites and customs and even to observe the Jewish law. "And all that was divinely given him through Moses he has full liberty to retain and uphold as far as possible when he becomes a believer in Jesus Christ."[21] Gaebelein and Stroeter further asserted that these converted Jews were not obliged to join any particular Christian denomination, but could form a congregation of their own in which they could retain their Jewish identity. This marked a great difference between the Hope of Israel mission and other Protestant missions to the Jews, including dispensationalist ones like the Chicago Hebrew Mission.[22]

While the leadership of the Chicago Hebrew Mission held a certain amount of respect for the Jewish tradition that kept the Jews waiting for the Messiah and regarded Zionism with enthusiasm, they did not advocate that converted Jews observe the Jewish law or create a congregation of Jewish believers in Jesus. Jews who converted through the missionary work of the Chicago Hebrew Mission were referred to a church of one of the many mainline Protestant denominations that participated in sponsoring the mission.

Gaebelein and Stroeter's attempt to create a congregation of Christian Jews was one of the earliest of its kind in the modern era. In Kishineff, Russia, Joseph Rabinowitz presided over a Jewish Christian congregation called Israelites of the New Covenant. Gaebelein, like other dispensationalist leaders in the United States, was acquainted with Rabinowitz and had even visited his congregation in 1895. He further translated into English Rabinowitz's *Jesus, King of the Jews* and published and distributed it as part of the Hope of Israel missionary effort.

The principles of the Hope of Israel mission attracted both praise and criticism in the premillennialist camp. Some of America's major premillennialist leaders looked favorably on Gaebelein and Stroeter's work.[23] James H. Brookes, for example, one of the outstanding leaders of dispensationalism in its early years, was delighted with the mission's work.[24]

Criticism of the policy of the Hope of Israel movement rose over the idea that Jews who have converted to Christianity could continue to be part of the Jewish people and observe the Jewish rites. Critics considered Jews who accepted Jesus as their Savior to have joined the church. They therefore considered the Hope of Israel attitude misleading and confusing.[25] The debate in the premillennialist camp over the incorporation of Jewish ethnicity and tradition, together with the belief in Jesus Christ as Lord and Savior, continued for many decades. Only in the 1970s did "Messianic Judaism," which adheres to the same principles that the Hope of Israel advocated in the 1890s, become dominant and normative for Jewish converts to evangelical Protestantism in America.[26]

The congregation of Christian Jews that Gaebelein and Stroeter organized did not last long. The new members of the congregation were in the process of penetrating into American society and climbing the ladder socially and economically. They did not remain in the poor Lower East Side. The attempt to create a congregation failed.

Our Hope, the mission's magazine, was published monthly. In its first years Ernest F. Stroeter edited the publication, which was intended both for missionary purposes and for raising support and donations among Christians. *Our Hope* regularly published articles dealing with developments in the Zionist movement, the new Jewish settlements in Palestine, and news from the Jewish world. Other articles dealt with prophetic hermeneutics of the Scriptures, developments in the premillennial movement in America and abroad, and developments in the field of missions to the Jews. The mission's organ published many articles of premillennialists in England and other European countries, dealing with the future of Israel. The mission also published a Yiddish version of *Our Hope*, *Tiqweth Israel*,[27] as well as a German version, *Unsere Hoffnung*.

In 1897, when the first Zionist Congress convened in Basel under the leadership of Theodore Herzl, Stroeter published Herzl's welcoming address to the congress in *Our Hope*.[28] A series of articles on various aspects of the emerging Zionist movement appeared in *Our Hope* as well as in other dispensationalist publications. Dispensationalists took great interest in the new movement and considered its emergence to signify the beginning of the events that would lead to the arrival of Jesus the Messiah and a sign and proof that history proceeds according to the dispensationalist prediction.

Gaebelein's first book, *The Messiah and His People Israel*, appeared in 1898. It was intended for distribution to Jews as part of the evangelization efforts of the mission. Gaebelein presented the dispensationalist interpretation of the past and future of the Jewish people in a manner that was meant to capture the hearts and souls of its readers. Although Gaebelein does mention the unpleasant elements in the future, such as "the time of Jacob's trouble," the overall tone of the book is extremely sympathetic to the Jews.

Hath God Cast Away His People?, published in 1905, was a collection of articles in which Gaebelein interpreted Paul's words on the future of the Jews in the eleventh chapter of Romans, as well as other biblical chapters crucial to the dispensationalist understanding of the future of Israel. *The Jewish Question*, published in 1912, is a shorter version.

The Hope of Israel mission opened branches in Baltimore, Philadelphia, Pittsburgh, and St. Louis. Its work was carried on outside America as well. A mission house sponsored by the Hope of Israel in New York operated for a few years in Jerusalem. The mission also conducted evangelization efforts in Warsaw, carried out by a Jewish convert whose conversion had taken place through Gaebelein's efforts in New York and who wished to go back to his homeland to preach the Christian message there to his brethren. The mission also made evangelization efforts among the Jews of north Africa and India.

The Hope of Israel mission started its work under the formal auspices of the Methodist Episcopal church. The actual involvement of the church with the mission was minimal and the mission was, to a great extent, free in its administration and in the formation of its principles.[29] The Hope of Israel received contributions from many Protestants who were not Methodists; in reality the mission was nondenominational. In 1897 Gaebelein concluded that the Hope of Israel mission no longer needed the official auspices of the Methodist church and decided to sever its formal connections and to declare it officially interdenominational. This did not mark any change in the actual administration of the mission, for the Methodist church had not intervened in Gaebelein and Stroeter's work.

The fact that the Methodist church gave its official support to Gaebelein and Stroeter's missionary enterprise for a few years, although it did not endorse its principles, no doubt derived from the realization that the mission's principles and methods were helpful in attracting Jews to Christianity. From that point of view, the Hope of Israel mission was in a similar situation to that of the Chicago Hebrew Mission, which was dispensationalist in its character but was nevertheless sponsored by a few mainline Protestant denominations with no dispensationalist inclination.

In December 1895 Stroeter delivered an address at the prophetic conference in Allegheny, Pennsylvania. Stroeter expressed his and Gaebelein's views of their role as missionaries to the Jews and presented many of the ideas that were carried out by the Hope of Israel mission.

Stroeter severely criticized the traditional Christian approach toward the Jewish people and, like other dispensationalists, blamed it for the unwillingness of the Jews to accept the truthfulness of the Gospel. It was only natural that the Jews had refused to convert when all they were offered by the Christian church was the view that they were no longer the chosen people and there was no hope for the reestablishment of the kingdom of Israel. Stroeter complained that Christianity wanted to strip the Jews of the very hopes and beliefs that had kept them alive as a people for so many generations in the midst of hostility and misery. In the field of missions the Jews had been treated as worse than heathens. Converted heathens were not expected to turn their backs on their people and give up their national aspirations, but converted Jews were forbidden to maintain any ties with their heritage.[30]

Moreover, Jews could easily have seen that, contrary to the traditional claims of the Christian church, the biblical prophecies that spoke about universal peace and the glorious future of Jerusalem had not been fulfilled. According to the dispensationalist hermeneutical scheme, those prophecies would be realized only with the Second Coming of Jesus. Stroeter emphasized the premillennialist conviction in the glorious future of Israel and cited chapter and verse from the Bible in order to validate this claim. He insisted that Jews who embraced Christianity had the right and even the duty to observe their customs and rites and to remain separated from Gentile churches.[31]

Like Blackstone, Gaebelein, and other dispensationalists, Stroeter praised Orthodox Jews who kept observing the Jewish tradition and expecting the Messiah. These Jews were the object of the premillennialist missionary zeal and were believed to be the Jews who would emigrate to Palestine and participate in the events that would lead to the descent of Jesus to earth and to the millennial kingdom. Stroeter criticized liberal, modern Jews who abandoned the faith and hopes of their fathers.[32]

Stroeter saw a new openmindedness on the part of the Jews in their attitude toward the Christian Gospel. He also recognized a more positive attitude on the part of Christians toward the Jews. In his view, the Jews had for a long time been not only despised but also neglected, that is, too little effort had been put into the attempt to evangelize them.[33] Like Blackstone, Stroeter saw it as his mission to arouse interest in the premillennialist camp in the spread of the Gospel among the Jews.

Stroeter criticized the traditional Christian views for stripping the Jews of what he considered their dominant role in God's economy for humanity, blamed Christians for treating the Jews as a rejected people, and called for a more appreciable and amiable attitude toward the Jews. But he also expressed some harsh criticism of the Jews in traditional terms. He accused the Jews of killing Jesus—"His own Son, whom, like all God's messengers, they rejected, and killed"—and explained the downfall of Jerusalem in 70 C.E. as God's punishment for that act. "God sent forth His armies and destroyed those murderers and burned up their city. Ever since that awful catastrophe, they have been scattered and driven among all the nations of the earth."[34] His criticism of modern Jews was expressed in harsh and disturbing terms: "a few decades of emancipation and equal rights and behold the unbearably proud and loud and obnoxious modern Jew, whose race-pride will yet fan the slumbering embers of inbred Gentile anti-Semitism into furious flame."[35]

A Fundamentalist and Premillennialist Leader

In 1899, Gaebelein abandoned his hope in the possibility of amalgamating the belief in Christ with the Jewish religion. He based this change of views on the dispensationalist hermeneutical system that distinguished sharply between Jews and Gentiles and assigned them different roles in God's plan for humanity. Gaebelein continued to hold the idea, so he wrote, that Jews did not have to join any particular Christian denomination when they accepted Jesus as their Lord and Savior. However, he became convinced that in this dispensation those converted Jews were no longer under the law, but rather under grace and should not practice Jewish rites.[36]

Gaebelein thus joined what was probably the majority in the dispensationalist camp in America at the time.[37] Stroeter did not change his views. He and Gaebelein parted ways. Stroeter settled in Düsseldorf, where he continued his missionary activity among the Jews applying the same methods and principles that he and Gaebelein had used in the Hope of Israel mission.

After the break with Stroeter, Gaebelein gradually withdrew from his missionary work. He continued his evangelization efforts for a few more years, but his work in this realm was limited mostly to the distribution of pamphlets and to preaching before Jewish audiences. Gaebelein called his mission in the years after 1899 the Gospel Mission to the Jews. The change of name manifested, to some degree, the change in Gaebelein's agenda. He continued to promote the Gospel among the Jews for some years more, but without the zest and high hopes of the early years. This change of attitude did not come because he was disappointed with his work among the Jews but because new activities occupied his mind. His attention was now devoted to his work as an evangelist and crusader of premillennialism and fundamentalism in the Christian Protestant camp. In 1904 Gaebelein ceased his work as a missionary to the Jews altogether.

As a crusader for what came to be known as fundamentalism, Gaebelein traveled extensively throughout the United States, preaching and lecturing. He also participated in biblical and prophetic conferences.

In November 1918 a prophetic conference took place in New York. The addresses reflected the deep impression that World War I and its aftermath, including the Balfour Declaration and the British takeover of Palestine, had made on American premillennialists. Gaebelein, speaking at the conference, interpreted those events as "signs of the time" that indicated that the present age was terminating and the coming of the Lord was near. Prophecy, he claimed, was being fulfilled and the ground prepared for the great events to occur.[38]

Gaebelein's main occupation now was the editing and publishing of *Our Hope*. The magazine that had started as the organ of Gaebelein's mission to the Jews became a publication dedicated to fundamentalist and premillennialist matters. In fact, it became one of the leading organs in the fundamentalist-premillennialist camp. It continued nevertheless to inform its readers of the developments in the Zionist movement and the Jewish settlement in Palestine. Gaebelein edited the magazine, which had a circulation of a few thousand, until his death in 1945.

Gaebelein wrote more than a dozen books devoted to biblical hermeneutics in which he interpreted biblical themes in light of his eschatological convictions. He dedicated other books to the promotion of the fundamentalist cause. Some sold thousands of copies, some tens of thousands.

In his writings Gaebelein manifested himself to be a hard-line premillennialist and fundamentalist. He saw the situation of humanity in his time as hopeless. Protestant Christian civilization had virtually collapsed as a result of the attacks of modernism, socialism, and all the other "isms" of the day. Gaebelein saw no remedy for the nagging problems of society but divine intervention in the form of the Second Coming of Jesus and his reign on earth. In this point he differed from his fellow dispensationalist William E. Blackstone, who believed that the imminent coming of the Lord and the approaching day of judgment should spur an attempt by the nations of the world to eliminate some of their major sins, such as wars, and suggested repentance and reform. Gaebelein on the other hand did not think that reform was possible. On one occasion, for example, he turned in his writings against temperance crusaders who rejoiced over their success of turning one of the states "dry." This victory, he believed, led nowhere.[39]

Gaebelein summarized his outlook in *Current Events in Light of the Bible* (1913) and *Hopeless, Yet There is Hope* (1935). He asserted that the political, economic, social, environmental, and moral problems of the age were becoming worse. "Down, Down, Still Going Down" reads the title of one chapter. But chaos would not prevail forever. Jesus would return to earth and usher in a new dispensation, the millennium.

In *Christianity or Religion* (1927) Gaebelein rejected the notion that he felt was spreading among liberal Protestants, one that gave legitimacy to other religions, placing them on the same level with Protestant Christianity. He lashed out against the higher criticism of the Bible and the academic discipline of history of religions, which he felt helped promote that atmosphere. Gaebelein manifested a knowledge of those academic fields and argued with their conclusions on their own terms. Christianity, he insisted, was not one religion among the many but the only valid conviction. Protestant Christianity, the fundamentalist leader argued, should not give up its claim to righteousness and superiority. As time passed, Gaebelein's writings reflected more and more bitterness, anger, and suspicion.[40] He had placed himself in stern opposition to the current trends in American culture. Whereas William E. Blackstone acted as a premillennialist inside mainline American Protestantism, Gaebelein, who was younger than Blackstone by more than twenty years, turned against the Protestant denominations that took the modernist-liberal line. He left the Methodist church in 1899 when he realized that this denomination was tending to accept the higher criticism, and he did not join any other denomination. Instead he prayed in an unaffiliated evangelical church near his home. Gaebelein belonged to the generation in which American Protestantism became divided into two camps: modernists and conservatives. He was an architect of this split and one of the leading spokesmen for the emerging conservative-evangelical camp. It was in this context of rejection of and anger at the entire world that Gaebelein wrote about Jews in a manner that has brought against him the accusation of anti-Semitism.

The *Protocols of the Elders of Zion*

In the 1920s Gaebelein published a number of articles in which he referred to Jewish involvement in the Bolshevik revolution in Russia. Gaebelein had criticized the Jews before and had directed severe attacks against specific groups in the Jewish nation such as Reform and secular Jews, but his words this time were more disturbing than usual. He apparently bought into some of the worst anti-Semitic accusations. Gaebelein repeated the claims of "white" Russian exiles that most (over 80 percent) of the leaders of the Bolshevik revolution were Jewish.[41] Jews' participation had indeed exceeded their percentage in the overall Russian population, but was far from the exaggerated role Gaebelein, following others, attributed to them.[42]

Gaebelein saw in what he considered to be the Jewish leadership of the Russian revolution a part of a worldwide conspiracy to destroy Christian civilization and overtake the entire world, a conspiracy that was put down in writing in the *Protocols of the Elders of Zion*.

Gaebelein accepted the authenticity of the *Procotols* and claimed that the plan indicated in them had already been carried out in part by the revolution in Russia and by such trends of thought and movements of the nineteenth and twentieth centuries as Darwinism, Marxism, and Nietzcheanism that came to undermine Christian civilization.

> Perhaps my readers may have heard of what are called "The Protocols of the Elders of Zion," which were given to the Public by a Russian named Sergius Nilus, in 1905. These may be genuine, or they may be forgeries (of course the Jews of Great Britain and the United States are vociferous in denouncing them as forgeries) but they certainly laid out a path for the revolutionary Jews that has been strictly and literally followed. That the Jew has been a prominent factor in the revolutionary movements of the day, wherever they may have occurred, cannot truthfully be denied, any more than that it was a Jew who assassinated, with all his family, the former Autocrat of all the Russians; or than that a very large majority (said to be over 80%) of the present Bolshevist government in Moscow, are Jews.[43]

In 1933, Gaebelein published his most controversial book, *The Conflict of the Ages, the Mystery of Lawlessness: Its Origin, Historic Development and Coming Defeat*. The book, which was well received in certain segments of conservative American Protestantism, was a bitter exposé of Gaebelein's severe critique of human civilization. In it he presented a picture of history as a conflict between good and evil, God and Satan. Gaebelein considered the

111

current age, whose most apparent calamities were World War I and the Bolshevik revolution, as a culmination of this struggle before the final battle in which Satan would be defeated.

In *The Conflict of the Ages*, as in his other writings, Gaebelein referred extensively to the Jewish people and repeated the paranoid accusations concerning the Jewish involvement in the Bolshevik revolution and the *Protocols of the Elders of Zion*.[44]

Gaebelein was not the only premillennialist who accepted, at least temporarily, the authenticity of the *Protocols*. Some other noted spokesmen of the movement like William B. Riley and James M. Gray, president of the Moody Bible Institute in Chicago, also considered them genuine documents.[45] There were premillennialists, on the other hand, who, from the beginning, realized that the *Protocols* were forgeries.[46] Some of them even went out of their way to repudiate them.

Was Gaebelein Anti-Semitic?

Gaebelein's words concerning the *Protocols of the Elders of Zion* have placed the evaluation of his thought and career in the center of an historiographical controversy. Wilson and Weber, who are critical of premillennialism, point to Gaebelein and to the other premillennialist leaders who accepted the authenticity of the *Protocols* as persons who have given legitimacy to anti-Semitism.[47] Rausch, who writes from within the movement, responded angrily to what he considered unjustified attacks against premillennialism in general and against Gaebelein in particular.[48] He views Gaebelein's interpretation of the *Protocols* as an exception to a career of a man who was, on the whole, a philo-Semite.[49] Rausch tries to validate his claim by pointing to Gaebelein's pro-Zionist sentiments as well as to his career as a missionary to the Jews.[50]

Gaebelein's attitudes toward the Jewish people are indeed complex and varied and cannot be judged solely on the basis of statements he made concerning the *Protocols*. Gaebelein, for example, had referred to Jews in some of his other writings in a manner and a tone that are extremely different from the ones he used in discussing the *Protocols*. In his autobiography, which was written at the same stage in his life in which he wrote about the *Protocols*, while describing the relief work he carried out among the poor Jews of the Lower East Side in New York, Gaebelein writes: "I could do just a little in paying back the debt we owe to the Jews. How could true Christians be heartless towards Jews?"[51] Elsewhere he wrote: "We forget that to this race—the race of Jesus—we owe our spiritual privileges."[52]

Gaebelein did not consider himself an anti-Semite. On the contrary, he expressed himself explicitly against that phenomenon. One time he signed a petition initiated by a fellow fundamentalist against anti-Semitism.[53] On a few occasions Gaebelein denounced the paranoid anti-Semitic accusations of ritual murder.[54] In doing so, he made use of his knowledge of rabbinical literature. Gaebelein asked his readers to purge themselves of prejudices they might have against Jews and look on them as people just like themselves.[55] Many years before Hitler's rise to power in Germany, Gaebelein wrote critically of his country of origin on account of what he considered to be its anti-Semitic inclination,[56] and he was an avowed opponent of Nazi anti-Semitism all along the way.

Contrary to Rausch's claim, Gaebelein's attitudes toward the Jewish people, Judaism, and Zionism as expressed in his writings on the *Protocols of the Elders of Zion* and in *The Conflict of the Ages* should not be regarded as an exception to his ideas on the matter or as a revolutionary break with them. Except for the acceptance of the paranoid idea of an international Jewish conspiracy to overtake the world, Gaebelein's writings in the 1920s-1930s do not stand in contrast to things he wrote previously. Nor do they reflect any contradictions or inconsistencies. In *The Conflict of the Ages*, for example, Gaebelein was expressing in extreme and bitter terms ideas that he had put down before. In this book, he is harsher, more bitter, more suspicious than in some of his previous works, but much of the substance is, in principle, the same.

The origin of Gaebelein's suspicious attitude toward Jews, an attitude that might seem on the surface to deny his more positive words concerning that people, can be found in his differentiation between various groups of Jews. Gaebelein held a certain amount of appreciation for Orthodox Jews, who regarded the Bible as divinely inspired and without error, kept hoping for the arrival of the Messiah, and prayed for the national restoration of Israel.[57] It was therefore the Orthodox Jews who would survive the Great Tribulation and reach the millennial kingdom, in which they would become the leading participants. At present, they suffer from "judicial blindness," which causes them to stick to the observance of the law instead of recognizing the Messiah. However, their eyes would eventually open to see the light.

Orthodox Judaism was, to a large degree, an exception for Gaebelein. It was the only religious manifestation aside from evangelical Protestantism for which he found any use and purpose. Although it was erroneous, it had a role in God's plan for humanity. Gaebelein not only rejected all religions except Christianity but he also expressed harsh criticism of all Christian groups that did not conform to his understanding of what true Christianity was. He rejected Roman Catholicism, Orthodox and Eastern Christianity, and dissenting Protestant groups such as the Mormons, Seventh-Day Adventists, and Christian Scientists.[58]

The Jews whom Gaebelein accused of leading the world into chaos, upheaval, and destruction were those who had abandoned traditional Judaism: "apostate" or "infidel" Jews, by which Gaebelein meant secular and Reform Jews, the latter of which he labeled "de-formed."[59] Like other premillennialists, Gaebelein had no patience for Jews who turned away from Jewish tradition. They would neither convert to Christianity nor await the Messiah and participate in the Jewish national restoration. They had chosen a road that led to nowhere but their own destruction. "There is nothing so vile on earth as an apostate Jew," Gaebelein wrote.[60] It was these Jews, who participated in numerous movements of social and political unrest and performed the atrocities of the Bolshevik revolution, who were capable of plotting to destroy Christian civilization and take over the world.

Antichrist and Zionism

Gaebelein addressed the events that, according to his belief, were to take place in the Great Tribulation, the period between the rapture of the church and the descent of Jesus to earth. In discussing the Antichrist who would be accepted by the Jews in the land of Israel as their leader he explained why Antichrist would be a Jew and not the pope, who had been traditionally regarded by Protestants as the would-be Antichrist. The pope, Gaebelein explained, did not deny the Trinity. He only claimed (falsely) to be Christ's vicar on earth. The Jews have better credentials than he as candidates to the throne of Antichrist. They deny the messiahship and divinity of Jesus Christ.[61]

One of the worst crimes the Jews would commit in their land at the time of the Great Tribulation, claimed Gaebelein, would be the rebuilding of the temple and the reestablishment of animal sacrifices therein. Although this development had been regarded as a necessary, inherent part of the divine plan for the end of days, after the true sacrifice of Jesus, the lamb of God, "for Jews to turn back to these sacrificial services which have no more meaning, is doubly obnoxious in the sight of God."[62]

In *The Conflict of the Ages* the Zionist movement as well does not escape Gaebelein's wrath. "The whole movement is one of unbelief which is displeasing to God, and finally results in new judgments upon Israel's land." While Gaebelein pointed to the developments in the Zionist movement and the Jewish settlement in Palestine as a sign that the coming of the Lord is near and the dispensationalist biblical hermeneutics is correct, he regarded the Zionist movement as no more than a necessary vehicle and rejected its secular character.

When Gaebelein had previously described the fate and role of the Jewish people in the years that would precede the descent of Christ to earth, in other of his many books and publications his enthusiastic description of the glorious future of Israel in the millennial kingdom had often overshadowed his gloomy prediction for "the time of Jacob's trouble." Similarly, in his treatment of the Zionist movement, Gaebelein's joy over what he considered to be a manifestation of the beginning of the eschatological events and the fulfillment of biblical prophecies had overshadowed other negative feelings Gaebelein held toward Zionism.[63] This time anger prevailed, and his attitude toward the Jewish people sharply reflected suspicion and rejection.

One should bear in mind that the tracts and articles that Gaebelein wrote in earlier periods of his life had been intended for distribution among Jews as part of missionary efforts. These writings naturally emphasized the more favorable apects of the dispensationalist attitudes toward the Jews. It might also be that when Gaebelein worked as an evangelist to the Jews, his attitude toward them was somewhat warmer and reflected a greater amount of good will and concern than when he wrote *The Conflict of the Ages*. By that time, he was no longer in contact with Jews.

Gaebelein had no connections with the Zionist movement. His support of the restoration of the Jews to Palestine was basically passive. He expressed approval and even enthusiasm for the phenomenon. But unlike his fellow dispensationalist William Blackstone, Gaebelein never went out of his way to help the Zionist cause, politically or economically. As far as the Zionist enterprise was concerned, Gaebelein was an observer, condemning its secular character and rejoicing at its achievements.

While Gaebelein's help for the Zionist cause was minimal or even nil, Zionism provided him with ample fuel for running his premillenialist engine.

He pointed to the Zionist achievements time and again as proof that the age is ending and the coming of the Lord is imminent. Besides the hopeless situation of humanity in general, Zionism was his only proof. The Jewish national revival and the resettlement of Palestine were an indication that the dispensationalist understanding of the divine plan for humanity was correct.

American dispensationalism has found in the building of the Jewish commonwealth in Palestine and the dramatic events that took place there a source of validation for its eschatological conviction. It helped dispensationalists sustain their belief in the imminent arrival of Jesus, a hope that has not yet materialized.

Gaebelein's Attitude Toward Nazism

Even before Hitler came to power in Germany, in 1933, Gaebelein had adopted an anti-Nazi line.[64] He rejected the Nazi theories, especially innovations in the realm of church and Christianity. He saw Nazism as an anti-Christian ideology and regime that, in the process of eliminating Judaic elements, stripped Christianity of some of its basic features (through such theories as the Aryanization of Jesus, for example). Gaebelein thus saw a connection between the anti-Semitism of Nazism and what he considered to be its anti-Christian attitude.[65] His premillennialist views served, in this case, as a wall against Nazi propaganda. The Nazis were altering the meaning of the Bible, which Gaebelein considered divinely inspired and which he insisted should be read literally. For Gaebelein, the recognition of the Jews as God's chosen people and the object of the prophecies for the end of time was an inherent part of the biblical message; to deny their place in the Scriptures was sacrilegious.

It was probably the use the Nazis made of the *Protocols* in their anti-Semitic propaganda that caused Gaebelin to abandon his belief in their authenticity.

Our Hope occasionally published details of the victimization of the Jews by the Nazis during World War II in Europe.[66] In this case Gaebelein's pessimism helped him grasp the full scope of the annihilation of the Jews. "If anything, the number of Jews killed is underestimated," Gaebelein wrote in reaction to one report.[67] Even before the annihilation of the Jews had begun, Gaebelein asserted that the Nazis' cruelties against Jews would be punished by God. "God will deal with the enemies of His people and when judgment comes, as it surely will, this modern anti Semitism will find its ignominious end."[68] In another article he wrote, "Poor Rosenberg, Streicher, Hitler and others, you are not fighting the Jews, you are fighting God, God's Son, our Lord, God's purposes and God's Word. What a terrible defeat and fate is awaiting you."[69]

With all his sympathy for the persecuted Jews in Europe, Gaebelein's concern remained passive. He did not come out with initiatives that were intended to help the Jews, such as petitioning the president and Congress to allow more Jewish refugees to enter the country, or calling on the president to put pressure to bear on the British government so that more Jews would be allowed to enter Palestine. Gaebelein's lack of initiative in this matter was not due to his old age. He did not even suggest such acts, for he was never in the habit of trying to shape or influence the course of events. His remedies for the calamities of the age were in the eschatological sphere.[70] In that point he differed sharply from William Blackstone, who had done his best to intervene on behalf of the persecuted Jews in tzarist Russia.

Conclusion

Gaebelein's writings reveal with sharpness and clarity the complexity and ambivalence of the premillennialist attitudes toward the Jewish people, Judaism, and Zionism. Gaebelein had shown at times good will and kindness toward Jews; he found interest in their culture and heritage, held appreciation for the instrumentality of Orthodox Judaism, and supported, not without reservations, the Zionist attempt to establish a Jewish commonwealth in Palestine. His attitude toward the Jews also reflected, however, mistrust, anger, and rejection. His prospect for the future of that nation included destruction as well as glory.

Gaebelein's recognition of the Jewish people as God's chosen nation and heir of the biblical promises to Israel for the end of days did not guarantee the elimination of prejudices. Nor can Gaebelein's rejoicing over the Jewish resettlement of Palestine be seen as respect for or trust in Jews. The pro-Zionist sentiments of early American premillennialists did not necessarily imply friendship or admiration.

Conclusion

The attitudes of American premillennialists toward the Jewish people, Judaism, and Zionism were marked by ambivalence and complexity. They recognized the Jewish people to be the heir of Old Testament Israel and the object of the biblical prophecies for a glorified, restored Davidic kingdom. Their eschatological scheme, as well as their system of biblical hermeneutics, designated to the Jews a place and a role in God's plans for humanity separated from that of the Christian church. This approach marked, to a large degree, a dramatic break with the prevailing traditional Christian doctrine that viewed the church as Israel and asserted that the role of the Jews ceased to exist after the appearance of Jesus.

Seldom before in the history of Christendom had such a large and influential group assigned so much importance to the Jews and to the prospect of their return to their land. Premillennialists considered themselves to have turned their backs on the hostility that had at times characterized the Christian attitude toward Jews and to have built a more favorable and appreciative approach in their relation to that nation. Premillennialists often expressed their regret for the mistreatment Jews had suffered at the hands of Christians and denounced the brutalization of the people whom they considered to be God's first nation. The efforts of William E. Blackstone in favor of the resettlement of the Jews in Palestine stand out as a striking example of the activity that the new interpretation of the role of the Jewish people in the eschatological happenings could inspire.

The attitude of fundamentalists-premillennialists toward Judaism and Jews, however, contained many elements that were not positive. Revealing a classical Christian outlook, fundamentalists often saw in the Jews the reflection of the biblical sinning sons of Israel. They expressed bitterness about the Jewish refusal to accept Jesus as Lord and Savior when he appeared for the first time, a refusal that in their eyes caused the delay in the materialization of the millennial kingdom. Although premillennialists denounced anti-Semitism, some of them at times expressed social, political, and economic prejudices in disturbing terms. Furthermore, premillennialists had little appreciation for Judaism. They considered the Jewish religion erroneous in its insistence on observing the law and considered the Jews therefore to be living in spiritual darkness. The only merit Judaism possessed, as far as premillennialists were concerned, was in its keeping the Jews waiting for the Messiah and the restoration of their national kingdom. It ensured their willingness to fulfill their role in the events of the end of age. Secular and Reform Jews, so dispensationalists believed, had abandoned these hopes and were therefore obnoxious and useless. Premillennialists insisted that only Christians who accepted Jesus as Lord and Savior could be saved. Jews who died without undergoing the act of conversion to belief in Jesus were, in their eyes, doomed.

Moreover, the dispensationalist prospect for the future of Israel is not necessarily beneficial for that nation. According to the premillennialist eschatological scheme, suffering and destruction await the Jewish population during the Great Tribulation, the period that would precede the arrival of Jesus to earth. Only one third of the Jewish nation would survive this turmoil and enter the millennial kingdom. At the time of the thousand-year reign of Jesus on earth, the Jews are expected to serve as the senior nation that conducts Jesus' administration. They would become, according to that view, the Brahmins of the millennial order. At the same time, however, they would be stripped of the religion and culture that they have built and kept for centuries. Their heritage would be lost.

The premillennialist attitude toward the prospect of the return of the Jews to their land and toward the Zionist movement was mostly instrumental. Premillennialists regarded the settlement of Jews in Palestine and the idea of establishing a Jewish state there as necessary steps in the advancement of eschatological developments. On the whole, insuring the survival and well-being of the Jews was not part of what motivated them in supporting these developments. They observed the movement of Jewish national restoration with much interest and joy. Although dispensationalism criticized the secular character of Zionism, they saw in it a fulfillment of prophecies and a confirmation of their understanding of God's plans for humanity.

Premillennialists, however, did not establish any organization whose purpose would have been aiding the Zionist cause politically or economically. Except for the activity of William E. Blackstone, the premillennialists' support for the Zionist movement was passive. They derived enormous encouragement from Zionism, but contributed very little to it. Instead, dispensationalists directed the deep interest they took in the Jews and the good will they felt toward that nation into the realm of mission. The evangelization of the Jews was the expression, par excellence, of the new concern premillennialists felt for the fate of the Jews. While some Jews sincerely converted to the belief in the messiahship of Jesus, many in the Jewish community resented evangelization attempts and considered them both an insult to their religious convictions and a threat to their national survival.

The premillennialist attitude toward the Jewish people and Zionism is relevant today. In the 1970s, after a few decades of keeping a relatively low profile, the evangelical-conservative segment of American Protestantism entered the public arena with much vigor and power. As was the case with the early fundamentalist movement, many of the noted leaders of the evangelical branch of Protestantism today are premillennialists. Among them are the leading evangelists of the nation: Billy Graham, Jerry Falwell, Hal Lindsey, Jimmy Swaggart, and Pat Robertson. Like their predecessors in the dispensationalist camp, they express, both in their writings and live evangelistic campaigns, their approval of the return of the Jews to their land and the building of a Jewish commonwealth there.

Like their earlier cobelievers in the imminent Second Coming of Jesus, they see in the building of a Jewish state a necessary vehicle for the advancement of the events of the end of the age. Whereas in the early decades of the spread of dispensationalism in America, premillennialists pointed to the first waves of Zionist immigration to Palestine and to the first agricultural Jewish settlements there as an indication that the Jews were preparing themselves for their role at the end of time and that the arrival of Jesus was near, today they present the birth of the state of Israel and its military victories and territorial expansions in such light. The Six-Day War, in June 1967, and its aftermath played an important role in that respect. More than the Israeli War of Independence in 1948, it raised the level of enthusiasm and the hopes of dispensationalists. They see the events in the Middle East as an indication that history proceeds according to their understanding of God's plans for humanity. The history of the state of Israel provides them with encouragement and hope.

While in earlier decades premillennialist support of Zionism was on the whole passive, the 1970s and 1980s witnessed an attempt on the part of American premillennialists to use their influence on American politics to promote the cause of the Jewish state. As the political potency of this segment of American Protestantism has increased dramatically, its voice is often heard when decision makers in Washington make their choices.

The official attitude of the Israeli government to the premillennialists is along the same lines as the reaction of the Zionist activists in America in 1891 and 1916-1917 to Blackstone's attempts to promote the idea of the restoration of the Jews to Palestine. Israel welcomes warmly and even encourages support from Christians in keeping with their eschatological hopes. In 1982, for example, Menachem Begin, then Israel's prime minister, decorated Jerry Falwell with a medal of the Jabotinsky Order, an organization associated with Begin's Herut party. Like the early leaders of Zionism in America, the Israeli leadership does not always see the connection between the aggressive missionary work premillennialists carry out among Jews and the political support they give to the state of Israel. Like Wolf Schur, the editor of *Ha-Pisga* in 1891, they often believe this support to be the only actual result of the Jewish role in the premillennialist messianic dreams.

The ambivalence in the premillennialist attitude toward the Jewish people, Judaism, and Zionism has also remained alive. The very same persons who give their political support to Israel and engage in other acts of good will and concern for the Jewish people, such as promoting the cause of Soviet Jewry, sometimes also express prejudice against Jews and their religion. A striking example was provided by Jimmy Swaggart, who supports Zionism and Israel and speaks about the glorious role of the Jews in the millennial kingdom. In one of his TV broadcast sermons in October 1984 he showed pictures from Auschwitz and other Nazi death camps in order to illustrate the awful fate that awaits those who do not accept Jesus as their Savior.[1] In doing so he demonstrated a premillennialist outlook that asserts that although the Jews are God's chosen nation, they would not be saved physically and spiritually until they accept the messiahship of Jesus.

Notes

CHAPTER ONE

1. On the background to the rise of premillennialist ideas concerning the Jews in England, see Barbara W. Tuchman, *Bible and Sword* (London: Macmillan, 1983), 80-101; David S. Katz, *Philo-Semitism and the Readmission of the Jews to England, 1603-1655* (Oxford: Clarendon Press, 1982).
2. For a recording of visionaries of Jewish restoration in Elizabethan and Stuart England, see Franz Kobler, *The Vision was There* (London: Lincolns-Prager, 1956); Peter Toon "The Latter Day Glory" in *Puritans, the Millennium and the Future of Israel*, ed. Peter Toon (London: James Clarke & Co., 1970), 23-41; Carl F. Ehle, "Prolegomena to Christian Zionism in America: The Views of Increase Mather and William E. Blackstone Concerning the Doctrine of the Restoration of Israel" (Ph.D. Dissertation, New York University, 1977), 47-61; Katz, *Philo-Semitism*.
3. On Brightman's ideas concerning the future of the Jews, see, for example, Toon, "The Latter Day Glory," 26-32.
4. Ibid., 32-34.
5. On the Puritan attitudes toward the millennium, see Iain H. Murray, *The Puritan Hope* (London: Banner of Truth Trust, 1971).
6. John Winthrop, the leader of the Massachusetts Bay Colony, wrote upon his arrival in the New World, "Thus stands the cause between God and us: we are entered into covenant with Him for this work . . . we shall be as a city upon a hill, the eyes of all people are upon us." John Winthrop, "A Model of Christian Charity," quoted in Perry Miller and Thomas H. Johnston, *The Puritans* (New York: American Book Company, 1938), 198-99.
7. William Bradford, the leader of the Pilgrims who settled in Plymouth, wrote, "May not and ought not the children of these fathers rightly say: Our fathers were Englishmen which came over this great ocean, and were ready to perish in this wilderness; but they cried unto the Lord and he heard their voice, and looked on their adversity." William Bradford, *History of Plymouth Plantation, 1620-1647*, 2 vols. (Boston: Massachusetts Historical Society, 1912), 1:156-58. Bradford's words echo those of Duet. 26:5, 7.
8. For a recording of manifestations of such creeds in seventeenth-century New England, see Ehle, "Prolegomena to Christian Zionism in America," 61-192. Cf.

Le Roy E. Froom, *The Prophetic Faith of Our Fathers*, 4 vols. (Washington, D.C.: Review and Herald, 1946-54), 3:19-143.

9. On Davenport's thought concerning the Jews, see Ehle, "Prolegomena to Christian Zionism in America," 67-69.

10. Ibid., 68. Davenport's knowledge of the Jewish response to Shabtai Zvi was not accurate.

11. Ibid., 69-73.

12. Ibid., 75-78.

13. Ibid., 74.

14. See Sidney H. Rooy, *The Theology of Missions in the Puritan Tradition* (Delft: W.D. Meinema, 1965), 230-42.

15. Ibid., 242-51.

16. Ibid.

17. On the background to the readmission of the Jews to England, see Peter Toon, "The Question of Jewish Immigration," in *Puritans*, ed. Toon, 115-25; Mel Scult, *Millennial Expectations and Jewish Liberties* (Leiden: E. J. Brill, 1978), 17-34; Tuchman, *Bible and Sword*, 121-46; Katz, *Philo-Semitism*.

18. On Edwards's treatment of the Jews, see Rooy, *The Theology of Missions in the Puritan Tradition*, 297-306; Ehle, "Prolegomena to Christian Zionism in America," 192-96.

19. See H. Richard Niebuhr, *The Kingdom of God in America* (New York: Harper, 1937); Robert T. Handy, *A Christian America: Protestant Hopes and Historical Realities* (New York: Oxford University Press, 1981).

20. Cf. Ernest L. Tuveson, *Redeemer Nation, The Idea of American Millennial Role* (Chicago: University of Chicago Press, 1968).

21. Joseph Smith, *The Book of Mormon*, 3 Nephi 20:29-33. Cf. 3 Nephi 29:1-4, 8-9.

22. Nephi 20, for example, discusses God's promises for building New Jerusalem as well as restoring the old one. Cf. LeGrand Richards, *Israel! Do You Know?* (Salt Lake City: Deseret Book Company, 1954); Truman G. Madsen, *The Mormon Attitude Toward Zionism* (Haifa: The University of Haifa, 1982).

23. For the story of Orson Hyde's mission to Jerusalem, see Eldin Ricks, "Zionism and the Mormon Church," in *Herzl Year Book*, vol. 5, ed. Raphael Patai (New York: Herzl Press, 1963), 155-58. See also Orson Hyde, *A Voice from Jerusalem: Or Sketch of the Travels and Ministry of Elder Orson Hyde, Missionary of the Church of Jesus Christ of Latter Day Saints to Germany, Constantinople and Jerusalem* (Boston: Albert Morgan, 1842), repr. in *Holy Land Missions and Missionaries*, ed. Moshe Davis (New York: Arno Press, 1977).

24. On Adams's settlement near Jaffa, see Reed M. Holmes, *The Forerunners*. (Independence, Mo.: Herald Publishing House, 1981); Mordecai Naor, "The Settlement of the Americans in Jaffa" (in Hebrew), in *Zev Vilnay's Jubilee Volume*, ed. Ely Schiler (Jerusalem: Ariel Publishing House, 1984), 343-50.

25. On details of occasional articles in Mormon journals on the Zionist movement and visits of Mormon delegates in Palestine while on tours around the world,

see Ricks, "Zionism and the Mormon Church," 161-74. One cannot, however, accept Ricks's thesis, which suggests a deep Mormon involvement in the fate of the Jews and the Zionist movement. Ricks's own exposé reveals how occasional and minimal were the Mormon referrals to Jews and Zionism. Ricks covers the period until World War II.

26. Cf. Tuveson, *Redeemer Nation*, 175-86; Leonard J. Arrington and Davis Bitton, *The Mormon Experience* (New York: Alfred A. Knopf, 1979), 36-37; J.F.C. Harrison, *The Second Coming, Popular Millenarianism 1780-1850* (New Brunswick, New Jersey: Rutgers University Press, 1979), 181.

27. See, for example, the treatment of the second coming of Jesus in Richards, *Israel!*

28. On Clorinda Minor and the colony she established near Jaffa, see her own account in a letter she wrote to Isaac Leeser in 1854. Reprinted in Moshe Davis ed., *With Eyes Toward Zion* (New York: Arno Press, 1977), 183-86.

29. For details on such groups, see Yona Malachy, *American Fundamentalism and Israel* (Jerusalem: The Institute of Contemporary Jewry, the Hebrew University of Jerusalem: 1978), 40-48.

30. See, for example, Clarke Garret, *Respectable Folly* (Baltimore: Johns Hopkins University Press, 1975); W.H. Oliver, *Prophets and Millennialists* (Auckland, New Zealand: Auckland University Press, 1978); Harrison, *The Second Coming*.

31. Tuchman, *Bible and Sword*, 175-207.

32. On the premillennialist thinking of activists of the London Society for Promoting Christianity Among the Jews, see Froom, *The Prophetic Faith of Our Fathers*, 3:415-33.

33. See Albert E. Thompson, *A Century of Jewish Missions* (Chicago: Fleming H. Revell, 1902), 93-106, 279-80.

34. It still existed in the 1980s, albeit in a more modest scope and without the zeal and fervor of the first generations of its operations.

35. On the history of such missionary efforts, see David M. Eichhorn, *Evangelizing the American Jew* (Middle Village, N.Y.: Jonathan David Publishers, 1978), 27-40.

CHAPTER TWO

1. Unless stated otherwise, premillennialism serves as a synonym for dispensationalism.

2. See "The Epistle of Barnabas," in *Early Christian Writings*, ed. B. Radice (Harmondsworth: Penguin Books, 1981).

3. See, for example, Arnold D. Ehlert, *A Bibliographic History of Dispensationalism* (Grand Rapids, Michigan: Baker Book House, 1965); Charles C. Ryrie, *Dispensationalism Today* (Chicago: Moody Press, 1965).

4. On Darby's life and career, see Clarence B. Bass, *Background to Dispensationalism* (Grand Rapids, Michigan: Wm. B. Eerdmans Publishing Co., 1960).
5. On Darby's thought, see Ernest R. Sandeen, *The Roots of Fundamentalism* (Grand Rapids, Michigan: Baker Book House, 1978), 31-41, 59-80.
6. John N. Darby to Prof. Friedrich A. G. Tholuck, *Letters of John Nelson Darby*, 3 vols. (Sunbury, Pennsylvania: Believers Bookshelf, 1971), 3:298.
7. Ibid.
8. Bass, *Background to Dispensationalism*, 55; Sandeen, *The Roots of Fundamentalism*, 31, 61.
9. "Historicist" is the term used by historians of American premillennialism. See, for example, Sandeen, *The Roots of Fundamentalism*, 36-39, 53-60, 62-64; Timothy P. Weber, *Living in the Shadow of the Second Coming: American Premillennialism 1875-1982* (Grand Rapids, Michigan: Zondervan Corporation, 1983), 9-10.
10. Based on Numbers 14:33-34 and Ezekiel 4:4-6, "each day for a year."
11. On William Miller and the prophetic hopes he created, see Froom, *The Prophetic Faith of Our Fathers*, 4:429-827; Leon Festinger, *When Prophecy Fails* (Minneapolis: University of Minnesota Press, 1956).
12. On Ribera and the emergence of futurism, see Froom, *The Prophetic Faith of Our Fathers*, 2:484-93.
13. On Darby's theory of the rapture of the church, see John Nelson Darby, "The Rapture of the Saints," *The Collected Writings of John Nelson Darby*, 34 vols., ed. William Kelley (Sudbury, Pennsylvania: Believers Bookshelf, 1972), 11:118-67. For a more recent exposition of the dispensationalist belief in the rapture, see John F. Walvoord, *The Rapture Question* (Findlay, Ohio: Dunham Publishing Co., 1957); Hal Lindsey, *The Rapture* (New York: Bantam Books, 1983).
14. Nondispensationalists have sometimes expected the rapture to occur at the end of the Great Tribulation.
15. Darby, "The Rapture of the Saints."
16. William E. Blackstone, *Jesus is Coming*, 2d ed. (Chicago: Fleming H. Revell, 1886), 65. Clarence E. Bass is wrong in asserting that "the church must be raptured out of the world before the tribulation because it is not a part of the kingdom, which will be in its initial stage of restoration through the remnant that survives the tribulation" (*Background to Dispensationalism*, 40). According to dispensationalist thinking, the body of the true believers would return to earth with Jesus at the end of the Great Tribulation, and it would be then that the kingdom begins. Similarly, Timothy P. Weber is not correct when he claims, concerning the rapture, that, "In this way the church would be removed from the scene so that God can resume his prophetic countdown and his dealings with Israel" (*Living in the Shadow of the Second Coming*, 21). Dispensationalists believe that not only Jews but Gentiles who are not part of the body of the true believers in Christ would also remain on earth after the rapture. The idea that

the true believers would be saved from the turmoil of the Great Tribulation had already appeared in Jewish messianic literature of the second temple period, as well as in such Jewish literature of later periods. See David Flusser, "The Reflection of Jewish Messianic Beliefs in Early Christianity" (in Hebrew) in *Messianism and Eschatology*, ed. Zvi Baras (Jerusalem: Zalman Shazar Center, 1983), 132-33. Opponents of the rapture theory are well aware that the idea that stands behind it is that the true believers would escape the Great Tribulation and build their arguments accordingly. See, for example, George E. Ladd, *The Blessed Hope* (Grand Rapids, Michigan: Wm. B. Eerdmans Publishing Company, 1960), 11.

17. The scriptural reference to the rapture of the saints is 1 Thessalonians 4:16-17: "For the Lord himself shall descend from heaven with a shout, with the voice of the archangel, and with the trump of God: and the dead in Christ shall rise first: Then we which are alive shall be caught up together with them in the clouds, to meet the Lord in the air: And so shall we ever be with the Lord."

18. In the mid-1970s, Dave MacPherson repeated this claim with much vigor. He claimed to have uncovered what he considered to be "the incredible cover up," namely, Darby's use of a vision of the secret rapture of the saints that a young Scottish woman named Margaret MacDonald had had in 1830, without giving her any credit for it. Dave MacPherson, *The Incredible Cover Up: The True Story on the Pre-Tribulation Rapture* (Plainfield, New Jersey: Omega Publications, 1975); Dave MacPherson, *The Great Rapture Hoax* (Fletcher, North Carolina: New Puritan Library, 1983).

19. See, for example, John N. Darby, "The Covenants," *Collected Works*, 3:44-56; James H. Brookes, *Israel and the Church* (Chicago: Fleming H. Revell, n.d.), 42-50; Cyrus I. Scofield, *Scofield Reference Bible* (New York: Oxford University Press, 1909), 20. For a more recent dispensationalist exposition of the subject, see Hal Lindsey, *The Promise* (Eugene, Oregon: Harvest House Publishers, 1982).

20. Ibid.

21. For a chart that illustrates the dispensationalist differentiation between God's plans for Israel and the church, see Clarence Larken, *Dispensational Truth or God's Plan and Purpose in the Ages* (Glenside, Pennsylvania: Published by the author, 1920), 19½.

22. C. H. Mackintosh, *The Lord's Coming* (Chicago: Moody Press, n.d.), 113.

23. For dispensationalist calculations of the seventy weeks in Daniel 9 see, for example, James H. Brookes, *Maranatha: Or the Lord Cometh* (St. Louis: Edward Bredell, 1874), 425-26; William E. Blackstone, *The Millennium* (Chicago: Fleming H. Revell, 1904), 59; Scofield, *Scofield Reference Bible*, 914-15; Arno C. Gaebelein, *The Prophet Daniel* (New York: Publication Office, "Our Hope," 1936), 135.

24. On William Miller and his attitude toward the Jews, see Malachy, *American Fundamentalism and Israel*, 21-27.

25. James Barr, *Fundamentalism* (Philadelphia: Westminster Press, 1978), 40-54; James Barr, *The Scope and Authority of the Bible* (Philadelphia: Westminster Press, 1980), 77-78.
26. Barr, *Fundamentalism*, 42. Barr gives as an example the fundamentalist interpretations of the creation story in Genesis.
27. Ibid., 190-207.
28. Cyrus I. Scofield defined dispensation as "a period of time during which man is tested in respect of obedience to some specific revelation of the will of God," *Scofield Reference Bible*, 5.
29. For a conscientious recording of the division of history in the writings of a few premillennialists, see Ehlert, *A Bibliographic History of Dispensationalism*. See also a chart of dispensationalist divisions of history in Ryrie, *Dispensationalism Today*, 84.
30. Based according to the dispensationalist belief on Jeremiah 30, Daniel 12, Matthew 24, 2 Thessalonians 2, and Revelation 7.
31. See Scofield, *Scofield Reference Bible*, 918. Scofield divided the seven years that separate, according to the dispensationalist belief, the rapture of the saints and the arrival of Jesus, into two periods. Only the second one, in his view, would be tumultuous.
32. Blackstone, *Jesus is Coming*, 65.
33. Detailed descriptions of the events of the end of days are found in almost all books that came to popularize the dispensationalist belief. See, among the most recent books, Hal Lindsey, *The Late Great Planet Earth* (Grand Rapids, Michigan: Zondervan Publishing House, 1971); Louis Goldberg, *Turbulence Over the Middle East* (Neptune, New Jersey: Loizeaux Brothers, 1983). For a chart that illustrates the order of the eschatological events according to the dispensationalist belief, see J. Barton Payne, *The Prophecy Map of World History* (New York: Harper and Row, 1974).
34. See, for example, Henry Ironside, *Who Will Be Saved in the Coming Period of Judgment* (New York: Loizeaux Brothers, n.d.), 12-14; Arno C. Gaebelein, *Hath God Cast Away His People?* (New York: Gospel Publishing House, 1905), 28-29, 69.
35. See, for example, Lindsey, *The Late Great Planet Earth*, 98-113. The dispensationalist image of Antichrist was based on Revelation 3, Matthew 24, and 2 Thess. 2.
36. C. Bass is mistaken in claiming that dispensationalists believe that only 144,000 Jews would survive the Great Tribulation and make it to the millennial kingdom (Bass, *Backgrounds to Dispensationalism*, 42). One hundred forty-four thousand is the number of Jews who would accept Jesus as their lord after the rapture of the church takes place and the Great Tribulation begins.
37. Premillennialists based their idea of the northern power on Ezekiel 38-39. See, for example, Thomas S. McCall and Zola Levitt, *The Coming Russian Invasion of Israel* (Chicago: Moody Press, 1974). For an exploration of the attitude of premillennialists to Russia since 1917, see Dwight Wilson, *Armageddon Now!*

The Premillennarian Response to Russia and Israel Since 1917 (Grand Rapids, Michigan: Baker Book House, 1977).

38. See Bass, *Backgrounds to Dispensationalism*, 29; Weber, *Living in the Shadow of the Second Coming*, 23; Malachy, *American Fundamentalism and Israel*, 133.

CHAPTER THREE

1. Brookes, *Maranatha*, 389-445.
2. James H. Brookes, *"I am Coming," A Setting Forth of the Second Coming of Our Lord Jesus Christ as Personal-Private-Premillennial* (London: Pickering and Inglis, n.d.); James H. Brookes, *Till He Comes* (Chicago: Fleming H. Revell, 1895), is almost identical to *"I am Coming."*
3. Brookes, *Till He Comes*, 81.
4. Ibid., 91.
5. See, for example, James H. Brookes, "Israel and the Church," *The Truth* 7 (1881): 117-20, 165-69.
6. James H. Brookes, "The Purpose of God Concerning Israel as Revealed in the Prophecy by Daniel," *The Truth* 9 (1883): 514.
7. James H. Brookes, "Salvation is of the Jews," *The Truth* 19 (1893): 331.
8. James H. Brookes, "Jewish Promise," *The Truth* 11 (1885): 211-14; "How to Reach the Jews," *The Truth* 19 (1893): 134-36; "To the Jew First," *The Truth* 19 (1893): 325-27.
9. Brookes, "How to Reach the Jews," 135-36.
10. Brookes, "Jewish Promise," 211-14; Brookes, "Work Among the Jews," *The Truth* 20 (1894): 15-16.
11. "Israel's failure was due to the fact that they refused to be separate from other nations, and hence they became disobedient to the word of God, and after a long and shameful career in unfaithfulness, and idolatry, and sore provocations of infinite grace and patience, they were finally disowned and rejected." Brookes, "The Purpose of God Concerning Israel," 502.
12. Brookes, "How to Reach the Jews," 135.
13. For a survey of the prophecy and Bible conferences, see Sandeen, *The Roots of Fundamentalism*, 132-61.
14. On the Niagara Conferences, see C. Norman Kraus, *Dispensationalism in America, Its Rise and Development* (Richmond, Virginia: John Knox, 1958), chapters 4 and 6.
15. "So many in these latter times have departed from the faith . . . so many have turned away their ears from the truth." Introduction to *The Fundamentals of the Faith as Expressed in the Articles of Belief of the Niagara Bible Conference* (Chicago: Great Commission Prayer League, n.d.), articles I, IX, V, VIII.
16. For a reasonable biography of Dwight L. Moody, see James F. Findlay, Jr., *Dwight L. Moody: American Evangelist 1837-1899* (Chicago: University of Chicago Press, 1969).

17. Note Dwight L. Moody's "The Second Coming of Christ," in Scofield, *The Second Coming of Christ* (Chicago: Bible Institute Colportage Association, 1896), 16-32.
18. Dwight L. Moody, *The New Sermons* (New York: H. S. Goodspeed, 1880), 535.
19. Moody was sometimes ambiguous, even when he discussed life after death. See *Heaven: Where It Is, Its Inhabitants, and How to Get There* (Chicago: Fleming H. Revell, 1881). Even passages in Moody's messages that can be interpreted as premillennialist do not necessarily carry a distinct dispensationalist attribute. Cf. Findlay, *Dwight L. Moody*, 410; Stanley M. Gundry, *Love Them In, The Proclamation Theology of D. L. Moody* (Chicago: Moody Press, 1976), 177-78; Sandeen, *The Roots of Fundamentalism*, 180.
20. Findlay, *Dwight L. Moody*, 253.
21. Cf. William McLoughlin, *Modern Revivalism: Charles Grandison Finney to Billy Graham* (New York: Ronald Press Co., 1959), 390.
22. See, for example, Dwight L. Moody, *Twelve Select Sermons* (Chicago: Fleming H. Revell, 1881), 118; Dwight L. Moody, *Glad Tidings* (New York: E. B. Treat, 1876), 105.
23. Dwight L. Moody, *"To the Work, to the Work!" Exhortations to Christians* (Chicago: Fleming H. Revell, 1880), 117.
24. Moody, *Twelve Select Sermons*, 113; Dwight L. Moody, *Great Joy* (New York: E. B. Treat, 1887), 454-55.
25. Moody, *Great Joy*, 456.
26. M. Laird Simons, *Holding the Fort Comprising Sermons and Addresses at the Great Revival Meetings Conducted by Moody and Sankey* (Philadelphia: John C. Winston Co., 1880), 221.
27. Moody, *Twelve Select Sermons*, 65.
28. See, for example, Dwight L. Moody, *Daily Meditations* (Grand Rapids: Baker Book House, 1964), 201.
29. Dwight L. Moody, *Overcoming Life and Other Sermons* (New York: Fleming H. Revell, 1896), 10.
30. Moody, *"To the Work,"* 118.
31. Moody, *Daily Meditations*, 48, 128.
32. Moody, *Heaven*, 13.
33. In Jerusalem the term "Pharisees" has often been used to describe extreme Orthodox Jews of European origin who are not Hasidic.
34. On this incident, see Naomi W. Cohen, *Encounter with Emancipation: The German Jews in the United States 1830-1914*, (Philadelphia: The Jewish Publication Society, 1984), 256. Moody's campaign in Phladelphia in the winter of 1875-76 was conscientiously recorded by a number of his followers. None of them gives any details of such an incident. See Edgar J. Goodspeed, *A Full History of the Wonderful Career of Moody and Sankey* (Ashland, Ohio: C. C. Wick & Co. Publishers, 1876), 261-406 (reprinted as *D. L. Moody in Philadelphia*, Hammond, Ind.: Helton Publications, 1975); Elias Nason, *The*

Lives of the Eminent American Evangelists Dwight Lyman Moody and Ira David Sankey (Boston: B.B. Russell, 1877), 125-53.

35. See, for example, Moody's denunciation by Rabbi Sabato Morais of Philadelphia in *The Jewish Messenger*, January 21, 1871.

36. See Moody's words in the *New York Sun*, vol. 43, no. 181 (March 12, 1876), front page.

37. H. B. Hartzler, *Moody in Chicago or The World's Fair Gospel Campaign* (New York: F. H. Revell, 1894), 96-101, 120-25; Richard K. Curtis, *They Called Him Mister Moody* (Garden City, N.Y.: Doubleday, 1962), 280-81. On Adolf Stoecker and his role in propogating anti-Semitism in Germany, see Franklin H. Littell, *The German Phoenix* (New York: Doubleday, 1960), 33-34.

38. Hartzler, *Moody in Chicago*, 101.

39. See Hartzler's account in ibid.

40. See, for example, a letter signed by J. R. to the editor of the *American Israelite*, December 10, 1875, discussing Moody's revival meetings in Philadelphia.

41. Cohen, *Encounter with Emancipation*, 256.

42. Moody, *Daily Meditations*, 72; Moody, *The Second Coming of Christ*, 31; Dwight L. Moody, "The Second Coming of Christ," *Northfield Echoes* 3 (1896): 281.

43. Dwight L. Moody, *To All People* (New York: E. B. Treat, 1877), 354.

44. Dwight L. Moody, *The Home Work of D. L. Moody* (New York: Fleming H. Revell, 1896), 67, 354.

45. Ibid., 355.

46. Robert E. Speer, *D. L. Moody* (East Northfield, Mass.: Northfield Schools, 1931).

47. Moody, *Great Joy*, 212-13.

48. On A. Ben Oliel, see Thompson, *A Century of Jewish Missions*, 178-79.

49. Florence E. Ben Oliel, "Palestine and the Jews," *Northfield Echoes* 1 (1894): 143-44.

50. Ibid., 147, 142-43.

51. George C. Needham. "The Future Advent of Jesus," *Northfield Echoes* 1 (1894): 498, 499, 496-97.

52. The story of the Spaffords was written by their daughter, Bertha Spafford Vester, *Our Jerusalem: An American Family in the Holy City, 1881-1949* (Garden City, N.Y.: Doubleday & Company, Inc., 1950).

53. Horatio Spafford wrote in his diary: "Jerusalem is where my Lord lived, suffered, and conquered, and I wish to learn how to live, suffer and especially to conquer." His daughter wrote that had it not been for the death of her father in 1887, the family might have returned to Chicago. See ibid., 56.

54. On the relationship between the members of the American Colony and the American consul in Jerusalem, see Alexander H. Ford, "Our American Colony in Jerusalem," *Appleton's Magazine* 8 (1906): 643-55, reprinted in Robert T. Handy, ed., *The Holy Land in American Protestant Life, 1800-1948* (New York:

Arno Press, 1981), 164-72. Sellah Merril was consul in Jerusalem in the years 1882-1885, 1891-1893, and 1898-1907.

55. Vester, *Our Jerusalem*, 134.
56. A statement to such an effect was made by the magisterial court judge to whom the various factions in the community brought their dispute. See Dov Gavish, "The American Colony and its Photographers" in Schiler, *Zev Vilnay's Jubilee Volume*, 140.
57. That is the attitude that Bertha S. Vester expresses in *Our Jerusalem*.
58. For example, Nathaniel West, "History of the Premillennial Doctrine," in *Second Coming of Christ, Premillennial Essays of the Prophetic Conference Held in the Church of the Holy Trinity, New York City*, ed. Nathaniel West (Chicago: Fleming H. Revell, 1879), 313-404.
59. William R. Nicholson, "The Gathering of Israel," in ibid., 222-40.
60. Ibid., 228-31.
61. Nicholson quotes Old and New Testament passages concerning that anticipated suffering. For example, Jeremiah 30:7: "for that day is great, so that none is like it; it is even the time of Jacob's trouble." Matt. 24:21: "Then shall be great tribulation, such as was not since the beginning of the world to this time." Ibid., 232.
62. Ibid., 233, 234, 235. Nicholson tried to substantiate his scheme by bringing in an abundance of quotations from the Scriptures.
63. West later expressed criticism of certain points in the dispensationalist belief.
64. Nathaniel West, "Prophecy and Israel," in *Prophetic Studies of the International Prophetic Conference, Chicago, Ill., November 1886*, ed. George C. Needham (Chicago: Fleming H. Revell, 1886), 122.
65. Ibid., 123.
66. Ibid., 124-35.
67. Romans 11:25-27: "For I would not, brethren, that ye should be ignorant of this mystery that blindness in part is happened to Israel until the fullness of the Gentiles be come in, and so all Israel shall be saved, as it is written. There shall come out of Sion the Deliverer, and shall turn away ungodliness from Jacob. For this is my covenant with them when I shall take away their sins."
68. William E. Erdman, "The Fullness of the Gentiles," in Needham, *Prophetic Studies of the International Prophetic Conference*, 56-57.
69. J. A. Owens, "The Second Advent Era in Bible Perspective," in *Addresses on the Second Coming of the Lord Delivered at the Prophetic Conference, Allegheny, Pa., December 3-6, 1895*, ed. Joseph Kyle and William S. Miller (Pittsburgh: W. W. Waters, n.d.), 66.
70. William G. Moorehead, "The Final Issue of the Age," in ibid., 10.
71. Edward P. Goodwin, "The Second Coming of the Lord, Personal and Premillennial," in ibid., 33, 40.
72. Robert Anderson, "The Principal Aims of a Prophetic Conference," in *Addresses of the International Prophetic Conference held December 10-15, 1901, in the Clarendon Street Baptist Church, Boston, Mass.*, ed. William J. Erdman (Boston: Watchword and Truth, n.d.), 12.

73. William G. Moorehead, "The Conversion of the World after the Conversion of the Jews," in ibid., 38.
74. Ibid., 43.
75. Ibid., 40.
76. Ibid., 44.
77. Leander W. Mundhall, "The Coming of the Lord and World-Wide Evangelization," in ibid., 109.
78. William J. Erdman, "The Structure of the Book of Isaiah and Part II. 40-66: A Prediction of Jewish History during the Times of the Gentiles," in ibid., 58.
79. Sholto D. C. Douglas, "The Antichrist: His Character and History," in ibid., 99.
80. William B. Riley, "The Significant Signs of the Times," *The Coming and Kingdom of Christ: A Stenographic Report of the Prophetic Bible Conference Held at the Moody Bible Institute of Chicago, February 24-27, 1914*, ed. James M. Gray (Chicago: The Bible Institute Association, 1914), 103.
81. Arno C. Gaebelein, "The Lord's Coming in Relation to Israel, Symposium," in ibid., 186-207.
82. Albert E. Thompson, "The Capture of Jerusalem," in *Light on Prophecy: A Coordinated, Constructive Teaching being the Proceedings and Addresses at the Philadelphia Prophetic Conference, May 28-30, 1918*, ed. William L. Pettingill, J. R. Schafler, and J. D. Adams (New York: The Christian Herald Bible House, 1918), 144, 152-53.
83. P. W. Philpott, "Coming Events Cast their Shadow Before," in ibid., 206-7.
84. Ibid., 12.
85. Reuben A. Torrey, "The Blessed Hope," 22, and David J. Burrell, "Signs of the Times," 69 in *Christ and Glory: Addresses Delivered at the New York Prophetic Conference, Carnegie Hall, November 25-28, 1918*, ed. Arno C. Gaebelein (New York: Publication Office, "Our Hope," 1919).
86. Arno C. Gaebelein, "The Capture of Jerusalem and the Glorious Future of that City," in ibid., 157.
87. William B. Riley, "The Last Times," in ibid., 169-70.
88. On the history of the *Scofield Reference Bible*, see Frank E. Gaebelein, *The Story of the Scofield Reference Bible* (New York: Oxford University Press, 1959).
89. For an account of the history of *The Fundamentals*, see Sandeen, *The Roots of Fundamentalism*, 188-207; George M. Marsden, *Fundamentalism and American Culture: The Shaping of Twentieth-Century Evangelicalism, 1870-1925* (New York: Oxford University Press, 1982), 118-23.
90. Arno C. Gaebelein, "Fulfilled Prophecy, a Potent Argument for the Bible," in *The Fundamentals: A Testimony to the Truth*, 12 vols., ed. Amzi C. Dixon, Louis Meyer, and Reuben A. Torrey (Chicago: Testimony Publishing Co., 1910-1915), 11: 60, 57.
91. Sandeen, *The Roots of Fundamentalism*.
92. The following is a partial list of these missions: The Chicago Hebrew Mission, 1887; Hebrew Messianic Council, Boston, 1888; The Hope of Israel, New York, 1891; Christian Mission to the Jews, Brooklyn, 1892; Brownsville Mission to the Jews, Brooklyn, 1894; Mission to Israel, San Francisco, 1896;

House of the New Covenant Mission, Pittsburgh, 1898; Immanuel Mission to the Jews, Cleveland, 1898; St. Louis Jewish Christian Mission, 1898; Hebrew Christian Mission to the Jews, Newark, 1904.

93. Charles Meeker, "Evangelization of the American Jew," *Christian Workers Magazine* 19 (1919): 868.

94. See references to specific articles that treated Zionism favorably in *The Institute Tie* and *Christian Workers Magazine* in David Rausch, *Zionism Within Early American Fundamentalism, 1878-1918* (New York: The Edwin Mellen Press, 1978), 164-86.

95. See Reuben A. Torrey, *The Moody Bible Institute Correspondence Department, Bible Doctrines, First Course* (Chicago: The Moody Bible Institute, 1901), 203-4, 208-11; Reuben A. Torrey, *Practical and Perplexing Questions Answered* (Chicago: Fleming H. Revell, 1908), 86; Reuben A. Torrey, "Jesus Christ—Notes on Lectures Delivered by R. A. Torrey," *The Institute Tie* 2 (1893): 48-49.

96. *The Mooody Bible Institute Correspondence Department*, 203-4, 208-11.

97. Reuben A. Torrey, *The Return of the Lord Jesus* (Los Angeles: The Bible Institute of Los Angeles, 1913), 68, 69-79.

98. James M. Gray, "God's Covenant with Abraham, or Why He Chose Israel," in *A Textbook on Prophecy* (New York: Fleming H. Revell, 1918), 18-26.

99. James M. Gray, "The War and the Jews," *Christian Workers Magazine* 16 (1916): 347-48.

100. See, for example, James M. Gray, "The Capture of Jerusalem," *Christian Workers Magazine* 18 (1918): 447; Gray, "Israel Restored and Renewed" and "Jerusalem's Capture in the Light of Prophecy," in *A Textbook on Prophecy*, 41-47, 200-206.

101. James M. Gray, *Great Epochs of Sacred History* (New York: Fleming H. Revell, 1910), 107.

102. James M. Gray, "The Jewish Protocols," *Moody Bible Institute Monthly* 22 (1921): 598.

103. The *Protocols of the Elders of Zion* were forged documents produced in tsarist Russia. The *Protocols* were used as anti-Semitic propaganda all through the twentieth century. On the emergence of the *Protocols* and their spread, see Norman Cohn, *Warrant for Genocide: The Myth of the Jewish World-Conspiracy and the Protocols of the Elders of Zion* (London: Eyre and Spottiswoode, 1967).

104. Ibid.

105. "God loves the Jews, men hate them. It was always so: men have always hated what God loved and loved what he hated," William L. Pettingill, *Israel—Jehovah's Covenant People* (Harrisburg, Pa.: Fred Kelker, 1905), 5 (reprinted in *Loving His Appearing and Other Prophetic Studies* [Findlay, Ohio: Fundamental Truth Publishers, 1943], 90-145). See also 69-70, where Pettingill quotes from Disraeli's "Defense of the Jewish Nation."

106. William L. Pettingill, *God's Prophecies for Plain People* (Philadelphia: The Philadelphia School of the Bible, 1923), 81; William L. Pettingill, *Nearing the End* (Chicago: Van Kampen Press, 1948), 50.

CHAPTER FOUR

1. From a copy in William Blackstone's personal papers in the possession of the American Messianic Fellowship, Chicago (hereafter BPP.AMF.).
2. On Blackstone's life, see, "William E. Blackstone—The Friend of Israel," *The Jewish Era* 1 (1892): 75-76; Cutler B. Whitwell, "The Life Story of William E. Blackstone and of 'Jesus is Coming,' " *The Sunday School Times*, January 11, 1936; "Their Works do Follow Them," *The Alliance Weekly*, January 18, 1936; Beth M. Lindberg, *A God-Filled Life: The Story of William E. Blackstone* (Chicago: American Messianic Fellowship, n.d.); Sandy Keck, "W. E. Blackstone, Champion of Zion," *American Messianic Fellowship Monthly* 78-79 (1973-74).
3. See, for example, Blackstone to Nathan Straus, January 2, 1920, BPP.AMF.
4. See descriptions of Methodist revival meetings in the following memoirs of Methodist revivalists: Peter Cartwright, *Autobiography of Peter Cartwright* (Nashville, Tenn.: Abingdon Press, 1956); James B. Finley, *Sketches of Western Methodism* (Cincinnati: Methodist Book Concern, 1854); Chauncey Hobart, *Recollections of My Life: Fifty Years of Itinerancy in the Northwest* (Red Wing, Minnesota: Red Wing Printing Co., 1885); David Sullins, *Recollections of an Old Man: Seventy Years in Dixie, 1827-1897* (Bristol, Tenn.: King Printing Co., 1910).
5. See letter of Ralph D. Smith, secretary-treasurer of the Bible House of Los Angeles, November 26, 1923, in Blackstone Papers, Moody Bible Institute Library.
6. See, for example, Blackstone's letter to *The Jewish Era* 11 (1901): 9.
7. Whitwell, "The Life Story of William E. Blackstone"; Lindberg, *A God-Filled Life*.
8. See William E. Blackstone, "How *Jesus is Coming* Came to be Written," *The Jewish Era* 30 (1921): 171-74.
9. See, for example, William E. Blackstone, *Jesus is Coming*, 3rd ed. (Los Angeles: Bible House, 1908), 20.
10. Sandy Keck, "William E. Blackstone, Author of *Jesus Is Coming*," *American Messianic Fellowship Monthly*, vol. 79., no. 6 (June 1974): 2-3.
11. For example, Blackstone, *Jesus is Coming*, 12-14. Blackstone begs the unconverted to accept "The Crucified Savior as the only hope of salvation."
12. Blackstone's stationery in the 1890s refers to him as "missionary evangelist," BPP.AMF.
13. On how the title of the book was chosen, see Blackstone, "How *Jesus is Coming* Came to be Written," 172.

14. See, for example, Blackstone, *Jesus is Coming*, 162-76.
15. William E. Blackstone, *The Heart of the Jewish Problem* (Chicago: Chicago Hebrew Mission, 1905), 16.
16. Blackstone, *Jesus is Coming*, 84.
17. For example, ibid., 122.
18. See William E. Blackstone, "The Jews," *The Jewish Era* 2 (1893): 134.
19. For example, Blackstone, *Jesus is Coming*, 171, 234-35.
20. Ibid., 222.
21. Ibid., 236-41.
22. Ibid., 174-76, 224-27.
23. Ibid., 226-27.
24. For example, Blackstone, *Jesus is Coming*, 167; Blackstone, *The Millennium*, 44; *The Jewish Era* 10 (1901): 55.
25. For example, Blackstone, *Jesus is Coming*, 238.
26. Cf. Weber, *Living in the Shadow of the Second Coming*, 141-42.
27. For example, William E. Blackstone, "The Jews," *The Jewish Era* 33 (1924): 87.
28. For example, William E. Blackstone, "Jerusalem," *The Jewish Era* 1 (1892): 70-71.
29. William E. Blackstone, "Missions," in Needham, *Prophetic Studies of the International Prophetic Conference, 1886*, 194-204; William E. Blackstone, *Satan, His Kingdom and its Overthrow* (Chicago: Fleming H. Revell, 1900), 36.
30. For example, Blackstone, *The Heart of the Jewish Problem*, 3; *The Jewish Era* 30 (1921): 5; "Jerusalem," 70.
31. Blackstone to Nathan Straus, January 17, 1921, BPP.AMF. On the *Dearborn Independent* and Ford's involvement in the spread of the *Protocols* in America, see Ralph L. Roy, *Apostles of Discord* (Boston: The Beacon Press, 1953), 43-43; Leo P. Ribuffo, "Henry Ford and the International Jew," *American Jewish History* 69 (1980): 437-77; Peter Grose, *Israel in the Mind of America* (New York: Alfred A. Knopf, 1983), 96.
32. Blackstone, *Jesus is Coming*, 162.
33. On the emergence of fundamentalism, see Sandeen, *The Roots of Fundamentalism*; Marsden, *Fundamentalism and American Culture*.
34. The mission still existed in Chicago in the late 1980s, under the name the American Messianic Fellowship.
35. See, for example, S. B. Rohold, *The War and the Jews* (Cincinnati: Standard Publishing Company, 1917).
36. David A. Rausch, *Messianic Judaism: Its History, Theology, and Polity* (New York: Edwin Mellen Press, 1982), 91.
37. Lindberg, *A God-Filled Life*; see Blackstone's reference to Rabinowitz in *The Heart of the Jewish Problem*, 12.
38. Arno C. Gaebelein, *Half a Century: The Autobiography of a Servant* (New York: Publication Office, "Our Hope," 1930), 53; Rausch, *Messianic Judaism*, 30-43, 78.
39. *The Jewish Era* 27 (1918): 44.

40. "To become a true Christian, accepting Jesus as Lord and Savior . . . brings not only forgiveness and regeneration, but insures escape from the unequaled time of tribulation which is coming upon all the earth." From Blackstone's speech at a Zionist meeting in Los Angeles, January 29, 1918, *The Jewish Era* 27 (1918): 44. Quoted also by Lindberg, *A God-Filled Life*, n.p.

41. *The Jewish Era* 27 (1918): 44.

42. "Their Works do Follow Them."

43. Blackstone to the Japanese ambassador in Washington, November 15, 1894, BPP.AMF.

44. See, for example, "Jerusalem," 70.

45. Lindberg, *A God-Filled Life*.

46. Felsenthal, born in Germany, served successively as rabbi of the Sinai and later of the Zion congregations in Chicago. A founder of the Jewish Publication Society and the American Jewish Historical Society, he was one of the few Reform rabbis at the time who were openly and wholeheartedly Zionist.

47. Bernhard Felsenthal to Blackstone, October 16, 1891, BPP.AMF.

48. Blackstone to Felsenthal, December 8, 1891, BPP.AMF.

49. See, for example, Felsenthal's complaint in ibid.

50. See Rausch, *Zionism Within Early American Fundamentalism*, 214.

51. See the list of contributors in *The Jewish Era*, all volumes.

52. Malachy, *American Fundamentalism and Israel*, 136.

53. Blackstone, *Jesus is Coming*, 211-13, 236-41.

54. Blackstone to President Harrison and Secretary of State James Blain, March 5, 1891, BPP.AMF; A. J. G. Lesser, *In the Last Days* (Chicago: N. Gonsior, 1897), iii.

55. On the conference, see George F. Magoun, "The Chicago Jewish Christian Conference," *Our Day* 7 (1890): 266-71; "Jews and Gentiles," *Daily Inter Ocean*, November 25 and 26, 1890.

56. "Jews and Gentiles," *Daily Inter Ocean*, November 25, 1890.

57. Magoun, "The Chicago Jewish Christian Conference," 271.

58. Ibid.

59. That Blackstone considered the petition to derive from the Christian-Jewish conference is clear from the way he presented himself at the end of the petition, as well as from his letter to Harrison and Blaine of March 5, 1891.

60. See his letter of January 28, 1891, to friends and colleagues in Philadelphia. More letters of introduction were given to Blackstone, for example, by F. Gerson, the editor of the *Chicago Israelite* (January 30, 1891) and by Rabbi F. De Sola Mendes (February 20, 1891), BPP.AMF.

61. On Adam Rosenberg, Hoveve Zion, and Shave Zion in America, see Israel Klausner, "Adam Rosenberg: One of the Earliest American Zionists," *Herzl Year Book* 1 (1958): 232-87; Marnin Feinstein, *American Zionism, 1884-1904* (New York: Herzl Press, 1965), 26-55, 80-93.

62. Rosenberg asked Blackstone to ask the secretary of state to put diplomatic pressure on the Turkish government to let Shave Zion register lands it purchased in the Golan Heights in its name. See Rosenberg to Blackstone, May

10, 1893, BPP.AMF. On the issue of the attempt to register the Golan lands, see Feinstein, *American Zionism*, 90.

63. *The Northwestern Christian Advocate*, April 8, 1891; Feinstein, *American Zionism*, 61.

64. Cyrus Adler and Aaron M. Margalith, *With Firmness in the Right: American Diplomatic Action Affecting Jews, 1840-1945* (New York: American Jewish Committee, 1946), 217-21.

65. Ibid., 217.

66. Grose, *Israel in the Mind of America*, 36.

67. Blackstone did refer to the non-Jewish population in Palestine in an article in October 1891 in *Our Day*.

68. Blackstone, according to one source, had sent a copy of the Bible to Herzl, but this was after Herzl had convened the first Zionist congress in Basel in 1897.

69. On the reaction to the memorial in the American public and especially in the American Jewish community, see Anita Libman-Lebeson, "Zionism Comes to Chicago," in *Early History of Zionism in America*, ed. Isidore S. Meyer (New York: American Jewish Historical Society and Theodor Herzl Foundation, 1958), 167-68; Feinstein, *American Zionism*, 56-79.

70. *Ha Pisga* 3 (May 8, 1891): 1. Quoted in Feinstein, *American Zionism, 1884-1904*, 61.

71. Feinstein, *American Zionism*, 64.

72. *Jewish Messenger*, March 13, 1891.

73. Feinstein, *American Zionism*, 73.

74. On Emil G. Hirsch's reaction to the Blackstone Memorial, see Libman-Lebeson, "Zionism Comes to Chicago," 167-68, 172-73.

75. *Yearbook of the Central Conference of American Rabbis* 45 (1935): 199.

76. See, for example, Kaufman Kohler, *A Living Faith* (Cincinnati: Hebrew Union College Press, 1948), 105, 159, 166, 210.

77. Kaufman Kohler, *Studies, Addresses and Personal Papers* (New York: Alumni Association of Hebrew Union College, 1931), 465.

78. Ibid., 454, 461, 463.

79. Kohler, *A Living Faith*, 165.

80. Kaufman Kohler, *Jewish Theology* (New York: Macmillan Company, 1918), 390-91, 395-96.

81. Kohler, *Studies, Addresses and Personal Papers*, 461-63.

82. Kohler, *A Living Faith*, 290; Kohler, *Studies, Addresses and Personal Papers*, 457-58.

83. David Polish, *Renew Our Days, The Zionist Issue in Reform Judaism* (Jerusalem: World Zionist Organization, 1976), 93-94.

84. Frank E. Manuel, *The Realities of American-Palestine Relations* (Washington, D.C.: Public Affairs Press, 1949), 71; Grose, *Israel in the Mind of America*, 40-41.

85. Dispatches, Russia, vol. 42, no. 87, the National Archives, Washington, D.C., uoted by Adler and Margalith, *With Firmness in the Right*, 225.

86. James D. Richardson, *A Compilation of the Messages and Papers of the Presidents*, 11 vols. (Washington: Government Printing Office, 1817-1898), 9:188.
87. Blackstone to Harrison, June 2, 1891, and December 3, 1892; Blackstone to Blaine, July 9, 1891; Blackstone to Gresham, December 7, 1891, BPP.AMF.
88. *Our Day* 8 (1891): 242-43.
89. Blackstone to Gresham, March 24, 1893, BPP.AMF.
90. Grose, *Israel in the Mind of America*, 40-41.
91. Blackstone to Earl of Aberdeen, October 18, 1894, BPP.AMF.
92. Blackstone to Cleveland, December 31, 1894, BPP.AMF.
93. Blackstone to Bishop S. M. Merrill, October 31, 1892, and November 10, 1892; C. I. Scofield's letters of December 19, 1892, and March 8, 1893, BPP.AMF.
94. A copy in BPP.AMF.
95. "It has been my privilege to revive the memorial on behalf of the Russian Jews, which was some years ago presented to President Harrison, and with the endorsement of the Methodist Preachers Meeting of Chicago, secured its presentation to President Roosevelt," *The Jewish Era* 12 (1903): 82.
96. The pamphlet also appeared as an article in *The Jewish Era* 1 (1892): 67-71.
97. There is no basis to Malachy's claim that Blackstone wrote the pamphlet "hoping to bring pressure to bear upon the anti-Zionism of the Reform Jews." Blackstone criticized Reform Judaism but had no hope of influencing it. Nor is it correct that "Orthodox Jews . . . had the pamphlet translated into Yiddish, and circulated 75,000 copies in the United States and other Countries." Although the pamphlet did not call for Jews to convert, Blackstone spoke openly in it about missionary initiatives. Moreover, it was circulated by Blackstone. Malachy did not read the pamphlet and based his claim on Lindberg's account. Malachy, *American Fundamentalism and Israel*, 138.
98. This might be also due to the fact that it was the shortest of his pamphlets dealing with the Jewish problem.
99. Quoted in Ehle, "Prolegomena to Christian Zionism," 250.
100. From the letter of endorsement attached to the memorial by Charles C. Bonney, president of the World's Columbian Exposition. October 19, 1893, ibid.
101. Among the American signers were Benjamin Harrison, John T. Morgan, chairman of the Senate Committee on Foreign Relations; James B. McCreary, chairman of the Committee on Foreign Affairs of the House of Representatives; Daniel Scott Lamont, secretary of war; Hilary A. Herbert, secretary of the navy; John D. Rockefeller; Marshall Field; and D. L. Moody.
102. The Hague Court of Arbitration was created in 1899 by the Convention for the Pacific Settlement of International Disputes. The court did not become permanent until 1920, when the League of Nations set up the Permanent Court of International Justice. The United States did not become a party to its "statute." It was only after World War II, when the Senate ratified the Charter of the United Nations, whose article 92 mandates the International Court of

Justice, that the United States became a party to the statute. Ehle, "Prolegomena to Christian Zionism," 253.

103. See, for example, Blackstone, *Jesus is Coming*, 104.

104. William E. Blackstone, "Britain Beware," *The Jewish Era* 11 (1902): 46-49.

105. Blackstone to the Archbishop of Canterbury, January 4, 1915, BPP.AMF.

106. *The Jewish Era* 29 (1920): 49.

107. See Blackstone's correspondence with missionaries in Eastern Europe in the 1920s-1930s, BPP.AMF (uncatalogued material); for example, his letter to Peter Gorodiskz, March 21, 1928.

108. Blackstone to J. P. Tumulty, Wilson's secretary, May 25, 1916, BPP.AMF.

109. In a letter to Woodrow Wilson, November 17, 1916, Blackstone wrote: "It would have been possible to have secured any number of signatures of the most representative character to the Memorial, but this was so evident that it was not necessary. The endorsement of the Presbyterian General Assembly, the Ministers' Meetings of the Methodists and Baptists, and many representative individuals and officials, evidence the general approval which the Memorial receives from our entire population." BPP.AMF.

110. *Minutes of the General Assembly of the Presbyterian Church in the United States of America*, new series, vol. 16, August 1916 (Philadelphia: Office of the General Assembly, 1916), 185-86.

111. Resolutions in BPP.AMF.

112. See Blackstone to Wilson, March 23, 1917, BPP.AMF. Later on Dr. Arthur J. Brown replaced Dr. Speer as secretary of the Presbyterian Board of Foreign Missions and as a member of the committee for presentation of the memorial to Wilson. Dr. Mott's name also was deleted from the list of members of this committee. See Blackstone to Wilson, June 14, 1917, BPP.AMF.

113. See Carroll to Blackstone, November 14, 1916, BPP.AMF. Anita Libman-Lebeson and Timothy P. Weber were mistaken in naming the Federal Council of the Churches of Christ in America among the Christian bodies that endorsed the memorial. Libman-Lebeson, "Zionism Comes to Chicago," 169; Weber, *In the Shadow of the Second Coming*, 140.

114. The Provisional Executive Committee for General Zionist Affairs was established in August 1914 to coordinate the activities of all Zionist groups and parties in the United States. The committee virtually absorbed the Federation of American Zionists.

115. See Straus to Blackstone, May 16, 1916, and Brandeis to Blackstone, May 22, 1916, BPP.AMF. "Your Memorial would be most effective if it derives its support from non-Jews," Brandeis wrote.

116. *The Jewish Era* 27 (1918): 44; Lindberg, *A God-Filled Life*.

117. See, for example, Eichhorn, *Evangelizing the American Jew*, 195.

118. Blackstone participated in the Zionist meetings in Philadelphia in July 1916 and in Los Angeles in January 1918.

119. See Wise to Blackstone, April 5, 1918, BPP.AMF.

120. At one time, for example, Marvin Lowenthal, director of the Provisional Executive Committee for General Zionist Affairs, asked Blackstone to publish

a Zionist propaganda article under his name. See Lowenthal to Blackstone, March 2, 1917, BPP.AMF.
121. The will was based on the assumption that the rapture would take place very soon. Blackstone believed that he and his family would be raptured from earth with all the true believers. In the meantime, until his return to earth, he wanted the Zionist movement to make use of his earthly possessions and commissioned Brandeis to be the trustee of the Milton Stewart Fund. Brandeis hesitated at first to accept Blackstone's will, but later consented. See Blackstone to Brandeis, April 18, 1917, and September 20, 1918; Brandeis to Blackstone, April 25, 1917, BPP.AMF. See also Brandeis to Blackstone, March 26, 1917, in *Letters of Louis D. Brandeis*, ed. Melvin I. Urofsky and David W. Levy, 5 vols. (Albany, New York: State University of New York Press, 1971-1978), 4:278.
122. See Brandeis to Blackstone, February 21, 1917, BPP.AMF.
123. The memorial was ready in May 1916, but Blackstone was still collecting signatures. He was ready to have the committee present it to Wilson in October, but Wilson was busy with his election campaign and was not in Washington.
124. See Wise to Blackstone, June 30, 1917, and September 17, 1918; Nathan Straus to Blackstone, May 16, 1916; de Haas to Blackstone, December 26, 1916; and Brandeis to Blackstone, February 21, 1917. BPP.AMF. See also Brandeis to Jacob de Haas, May 8, 1917, June 7, 1917, and December 6, 1917, *Letters of Louis D. Brandeis*, 4:289, 296, 327.
125. Wise to Blackstone, June 30, 1917, and September 17, 1918, BPP.AMF.
126. Historians who have not gone through Blackstone's personal papers mistakenly thought that Blackstone submitted the petition. See, for example, Liebman-Lebeson, "Zionism comes to Chicago," 163; Malachy, *American Fundamentalism and Israel*, 139; Lawrence J. Epstein, *Zion's Call, Christian Contributions to the Origins and Development of Israel* (Lanham, Md.: University Press of America, 1984), 112.
127. See Blackstone to Stephen Wise, July 9, 1917, BPP.AMF.
128. In his letter to Blackstone of June 30, 1917, Stephen Wise wrote: "I had the honor of presenting in informal fashion to the President at the White House yesterday a copy of your petition. The President accepted it, but he felt that this was not the best time for the public or private presentation thereof. I think I have the right to say that the President is prepared to leave to Justice Brandeis the decision with respect to the most opportune time in which formally to present the petition to him." BPP.AMF. Wise refers to his meeting with Wilson in his autobiography, *Challenging Years* (New York: G.P. Putnam's Sons, 1949), p. 189, but does not mention Blackstone and his petition.
   Bashford, one of the people to whom Blackstone entrusted the presentation of the petition, wrote to Blackstone two days afterward and told him that: "the whole matter of a public hearing depends upon President Wilson. At times he seems to want the public hearing and at other times he requests it to be postponed." BPP.AMF.

129. See Robert Speers to Blackstone, May 23, 1917, and Bashford to Blackstone, June 1, 1917, BPP.AMF. Wilson discussed changes with Brandeis. His specific request was to drop the suggestion to put the future Jewish commonwealth in Palestine under "international control," and leave the control "undesignated." Brandeis was in favour of the same changes. See Brandeis to Jacob de Haas, May 8, 1917, *Letters of Louis D. Brandeis*, 4:289. Brandeis obviously discussed the petition in detail with Wilson.

130. At one time Wilson sent Henry J. Morgenthau to the Middle East to try and persuade Turkey to sign a separate peace treaty with the Entente Powers. The British, who were eager to conquer Turkish territories, sent Chaim Weizmann to persuade Morgenthau to abandon his mission. Wilson was aware of Britain's attempt to use her promise to build a Jewish home in Palestine as a means to put her hands on Palestine. Although he favored the Zionist idea, Wilson hesitated at first to give his approval to the issuing of the Balfour Declaration. See Leonard Stein, *The Balfour Declaration* (London: Valentine, Mitchell and Co., 1961), 529; Grose, *Israel in the Mind of America*, 61-62.

131. See Grose, *Israel in the Mind of America*, 60-63. Cf. Stein, *The Balfour Declaration*, 530.

132. Cf. Ben Halpern, *A Clash of Heroes* (New York: Oxford University Press, 1987), 168.

133. See, for example, Stein, *The Balfour Declaration*; Isaiah Friedman, *The Question of Palestine, 1914-1918, British-Jewish-Arab Relations* (London: Routledge & Kegan Paul, 1973).

134. "He never once mentioned the Second Coming, and he always said that we need not worry about heaven—that would take care of itself—but had to be concerned about the problems of this world." Arthur S. Link, Wilson's biographer and editor of his papers, to Y. Ariel, July 18, 1984.

135. Wise, *Challenging Years*, 186-87.

136. Manuel, *The Realities of American-Palestine Relations*, 256-57.

137. See Joseph L. Grabill, *Protestant Diplomacy and the Near East: Missionary Influence on American Policy, 1810-1927* (Minneapolis: University of Minnesota Press, 1971). Grabill deals mostly with the missionaries' attempt to influence the Wilson administration.

138. On Dodge's connection with Wilson, see ibid., 80-93.

139. Wilson was not impressed by the efforts of the pro-Arab lobby and remained committed to his pro-Zionist promises. See, for example, ibid., 178.

140. See, for example, Blackstone, *Jesus is Coming*, 208-9.

141. Blackstone predicted that the end would occur by 1933. "Jewish Restoration Past and Present," *The Jewish Era* 32 (1923): 11-12; *The "Times of the Gentiles" and the Time of the End* (Chicago: Fleming H. Revell Co., n.d. [1921]), 14. Blackstone had predicted a date for the establishment of the millennial kingdom back in 1893, *The Jewish Era* 2 (1893): 238-41. But then he predicted the date 1972, which was safely far ahead. In 1923, as a consequence of World War I and the Balfour Declaration, he risked predicting a very close date.

142. Blackstone was aware of the danger in predicting a specific date for the Second Coming of Jesus. *The "Times of the Gentiles" and the Time of the End*, 1.

143. Blackstone, *Jesus is Coming*, 240; Blackstone, *The "Times of the Gentiles" and the Time of the End*, 18-19. There is no basis for Malachy's claim that "in the last years of his life, disappointment at the secular character of Zionism and an intensification of his missionary strivings may be detected," *American Fundamentalism and Israel*, 141. Blackstone was an active missionary to the Jews and criticized the secular character of Zionism all along the way.

144. See Blackstone, *The Heart of the Jewish Problem*.

145. Grose, *Israel in the Mind of America*, 36. This copy of the Bible is currently on display at the Herzl Museum in Mount Herzl, Jerusalem.

146. See, for example, Blackstone to W. Wilson, March 29, 1917, BPP.AMF.

147. *The Jewish Era* 17 (1918): 80-82.

148. Blackstone to Wilson, November 4, 1914. In a telegram to Warren G. Harding, December 30, 1920, Blackstone wrote: "God has reserved our nation for special service in the impending crux of human history. Isaiah Eighteen." BPP.AMF.

149. See, for example, *The Jewish Era* 26 (1917): 5-6. On Blackstone's interpretation of World War I, see Ehle, "Prolegomena to Christian Zionism in America," 290-302.

150. *Encyclopedia Judaica*, s.v. "Christian Zionism"; *Encyclopedia of Zionism and Israel*, ed. Raphael Patai (New York: Herzl Press/McGraw-Hill, 1971), s.v. "Restoration Movement"; Ehle, "Prolegomena to Christian Zionism in America," 339-45; Epstein, *Zion's Call*; Michael J. Pragai, *Faith and Fulfillment, Christians and the Return to the Promised Land* (London: Valentine, Mitchell and Company, 1985).

151. Ehle, "Prolegomena to Christian Zionism in America," 339.

152. Kobler, *The Vision was There*, 9-10, 117-18.

CHAPTER FIVE

1. Gaebelein, *Half a Century*.
2. Ibid., 1.
3. Cf. ibid., 28.
4. Ibid., 32.
5. See "First Annual Report," *Our Hope* 1 (1894): 19.
6. See Gaebelein, *Half a Century*, 27-28.
7. *Our Hope* 1 (1894): 18.
8. See, for example, Eichhorn, *Evangelizing the American Jew*; Tuchman, *Bible and Sword*, 183-89.
9. See, for example, Arno C. Gaebelein, *The Messiah and His People Israel* (New York: Hope of Israel, 1898), 50-51.
10. "Notes from our Mission," *Our Hope* 1 (1894): 24.

11. See, for example, Samuel Freuder, *My Return to Judaism* (New York: B. Zuckerman, 1922).
12. Gaebelein, *Half a Century*, 29.
13. For example, Arno C. Gaebelein, "Herman Warszwiak's Method of Getting Crowds to Hear the Gospel," *Our Hope* 2 (1895): 2-5.
14. Gaebelein, *Half a Century*, 29.
15. Eichhorn, *Evangelizing the American Jew*.
16. Gaebelein, *Half a Century*, 30.
17. See Samuel Wilkinson, "The Moral Defensibility of some of the Methods Employed in Jewish Missions," *Yearbook of the Evangelical Missions Among the Jews*, ed. Hermann L. Strack, 2 vols. (Leipzig: J. C. Hinrichs'sche Buchhandlung, 1906-1913), 1:60-67.
18. See Eichhorn's description of Jacob Freshman, Hermann Warszawiak, and Leopold Cohn in *Evangelizing the American Jew*, 163-65, 167-76, 195.
19. Ernest F. Stroeter, "Christ's Second Coming Premillienial" in Needham, *Prophetic Studies of the International Prophetic Conference, 1886*, 16.
20. Ibid., 17. In describing Stroeter's address, Rausch refers only to this part of Stroeter's speech and does not mention the earlier part in which Stroeter criticizes Israel's rejection of Jesus. David A. Rausch, *Arno C. Gaebelein, 1861-1945: Irenic Fundamentalist and Scholar* (New York: Edwin Mellen Press, 1983), 9-10.
21. From "The Principles of the Hope of Israel Movement," in Gaebelein, *The Messiah and His People Israel*, 65.
22. There is, however, no basis to Rausch's claim that, "The Jewish community, although opposed to Gentile missionary enterprises to the Jews, sensed that there was something different about this mission," *Arno C. Gaebelein, 1861-1945*, 10. Most Jews could not tell the difference between the ideology of one Protestant mission and another. As far as the Jewish community was concerned, all missionaries were out to capture Jewish souls.
23. Gaebelein, *Half a Century*, 39-45.
24. Brookes, "Work among the Jews."
25. For the response of the Hope of Israel mision to such criticism, see Ernest F. Stroeter, "A Misapprehension Corrected," *Our Hope* 2 (1895): 55-58.
26. Rausch, *Messianic Judaism*.
27. Rausch is mistaken in asserting that *Tiqweth Israel* was written in Hebrew, *Arno C. Gaebelein, 1861-1945*, 8.
28. "Address of Welcome to the Zionist Congress," *Our Hope* 3 (1897): 130-34.
29. Arno C. Gaebelein, "A Very Important Announcement," *Our Hope* 3 (1897): 356; Arno C. Gaebelein, "How the Hope of Israel became Undenominational," *Our Hope* 4 (1897): 3-5.
30. Ernest F. Stroeter, "The Second Coming of Christ in Relation to Israel," in Kyle and Miller, *Addresses on the Second Coming of the Lord*, 136-56.
31. Ibid., 137, 148, 151-56.
32. Ibid., 139, 140.

33. Ibid., 136.
34. Ibid., 138. David Rausch, who analyzes thoroughly Stroeter's address, neglects that part of his speech. *Arno C. Gabelein, 1861-1945*, 27-30.
35. Stroeter, "The Second Coming of Christ," 139.
36. Arno C. Gaebelein, "A Short Review of Our Mission and the Principles of the Hope of Israel Movement," *Our Hope* 6 (1899): 68-71.
37. Rausch, *Messianic Judaism*, chaps. 3 and 4.
38. Gaebelein, "The Capture of Jerusalem," 145-60.
39. Marsden considers Gaebelein one of the extreme condemners of the age among pre-World War I premillennialists, *Fundamentalism and American Culture*, 124-32.
40. Rausch tries to draw a portrait of Gaebelein as an amicable, broadminded person. This attempt, based on the memories of his son Frank, cannot be corroborated when we see the reflections of Gaebelein's temperament in his writings. See *Arno C. Gaebelein, 1861-1945*.
41. For example, Arno C. Gaebelein, "Jewish Leadership in Russia," *Our Hope* 27 (1921): 734-35.
42. On the evident influence of "white" Russian writings on shaping Gaebelein's outlooks on this issue, see Arno C. Gaebelein, *The Conflict of the Ages* (New York: Publication Office, "Our Hope," 1933), 95-98. Rausch, who detailed the sources of information that had nourished Gaebelein's views on the matter, had overlooked the "white" Russian sources, *Arno C. Gaebelein, 1861-1945*, 147.
43. Arno C. Gaebelein, "Isaiah Chapter XIX, The Conversion of Egypt" *Our Hope*, 27 (1921): 601. See also Gaebelein, "Jewish Leadership in Russia," 734-35; Arno C. Gaebelein, "Aspects of Jewish Power in the United States," *Our Hope* 29 (1922): 103. The passage quoted is the only one in which Gaebelein mentions the possibility that the *Protocols* are forgeries. He tends to treat them here, however, as genuine documents.
44. Gaebelein, *The Conflict of the Ages*, 95-100.
45. Gray, "The Jewish Protocols"; William B. Riley, *Wanted—A World Leader!* (Published by the author, n.d.), 41-51, 71-72.
46. Roy, *Apostles of Discord*, 45-46.
47. Dwight Wilson writes that Gaebelein "seemed to provide legitimacy for the Nazi attitude." *Armageddon Now!*, 97. Timothy P. Weber is more moderate and careful than Wilson in his evaluation of the phenomenon. He writes that "at times premillennialists sounded anti-Semitic" and "some leaders of the movement acted like representatives of American anti-Semitism." On Gaebelein specifically, he says, "by giving credence to tales of international Jewish conspiracies, he affirmed many of the arguments that anti-Semites used to justify their war against the Jews. In that way, Gaebelein was giving unintentional ideological support to the forces of anti Semitism." *Living in the Shadow of the Second Coming*, 154, 188.
48. See Rausch and Weber's debate: David A. Rausch, "Fundamentalism and the Jew: An Interpretive Essay," *Journal of the Evangelical Theological Society* 23

(1980): 102-12; Timothy P. Weber, "A Reply to David Rausch's 'Fundamentalism and the Jew,'" *Journal of the Evangelical Theological Society* 24 (1981):67-71; David A. Rausch, "A Rejoinder to Timothy Weber's Reply," *Journal of the Evangelical Theological Society* 24 (1981): 73-77; Timothy P. Weber, "A Surrejoinder to David Rausch's Rejoinder," *Journal of the Evangelical Theological Society* 24 (1981): 79-82.

49. For example, Rausch, *Arno C. Gaebelein, 1861-1945*, 130-31.

50. Rausch adopts at times an overwhelmingly apologetic line in his defense of Gaebelein. Although his basic thesis that Gaebelein should not be labeled an anti-Semite is on the whole correct, many of the arguments he used to build his claim cannot be accepted. See, for example, Rausch's explanation for Gaebelein's "the Jew Trotsky," ibid., 145-46.

51. Gaebelein, *Half a Century*, 35.

52. Arno C. Gaebelein, "The Middle Wall of Partition," *Our Hope* 34 (June 1928): 750.

53. Roy, *Apostles of Discord*, 379.

54. See, for example, Arno C. Gaebelein, "The Same Old Accusation," *Our Hope* 30 (1924): 556.

55. ". . . just folks like ourselves, resentful of injustice, responsive to kindness, sensitive to disdain." "The Middle Wall of Partition."

56. See "First Letter of Mr. Gaebelein," *Our Hope* 2 (1895): 78.

57. Gaebelein, *The Conflict of the Ages*, 147.

58. See, for example, Arno C. Gaebelein, *Current Events in the Light of the Bible* (New York: Publication Office, "Our Hope," 1914), 58, 67-68, 98; Gaebelein, *Half a Century*, 177, 228, 235-36.

59. Gaebelein, *The Conflict of the Ages*, 147.

60. Gaebelein, "Aspects of Jewish Power in the United States."

61. In earlier writings Gaebelein gave another explanation: "As Jesus Christ was a Jew, so, counterfeiting as far as possible, Satan may use an apostate Jew for his Antichrist," *The Messiah and His People, Israel*, 45. Cf. Weber, *Living in the Shadow of the Second Coming*, 154.

62. Gaebelein, *The Conflict of the Ages*, 151.

63. See, for example, Gaebelein, *Hath God Cast Away His People?*, 181-204.

64. Arno C. Gaebelein, "Adolf Hitler—Will He Be Germany's Dictator?" *Our Hope* 37 (1930):363-64; Arno C. Gaebelein, "The Shadows of Jacob's Trouble," *Our Hope* 38 (1932): 102.

65. See, for example, *Our Hope* 44 (1938): 686.

66. For a detailed survey of *Our Hope*'s publications on the Holocaust, see David A. Rausch, "Our Hope: An American Fundamentalist Journal and the Holocaust, 1937-1945," *Fides et Historia* 12 (1980): 89-103.

67. Arno C. Gaebelein, "The New Great World Crisis: XXIII," *Our Hope* 49 (1943): 815.

68. Arno C. Gaebelein, "The Plight of the Austrian Jews," *Our Hope* 44 (1938): 825-26.

69. Arno C. Gaebelein, "Alfred Rosenberg, the German Anti-Christian Leader Speaks Again," *Our Hope* 45 (1939): 689.
70. In discussing the situation in Nazi Germany in 1938, Gaebelein concludes: "How long oh Lord? How Long? Till He comes." "Observations and Experiences," *Our Hope* 44 (1938): 750.

CONCLUSION

1. Ruth W. Mouly, *The Religious Right and Israel: The Politics of Armageddon* (Chicago: Midwest Research, 1985), 23.

Bibliography

PRIMARY SOURCES

Archival Material

Blackstone, William E. Personal Papers. Moody Bible Institute Library, Chicago, Illinois. File C.B. B631.
Blackstone, William E. Personal Papers. American Messianic Fellowship. Chicago, Illinois. Uncatalogued.

Published Sources

Anderson, Robert. "The Principal Aims of a Prophetic Conference." In Erdman, *Addresses of the International Prophetic Conference 1901.*
Barnabas. "The Epistle of Barnabas." In *Early Christian Writings.* Trans. M. Stainforth. Edited by B. Radice. Harmondsworth: Penguin Books, 1981.
Ben Oliel, Florence E. "Palestine and the Jews." *Northfield Echoes* 1 (1894): 142-46.
Blackstone, William E. *Jesus is Coming.* 1st ed. Chicago: Fleming H. Revell, 1878; 2d ed. Chicago: Fleming H. Revell, 1886. 3d ed. Los Angeles: Bible House, 1908. *Hofaat Ha-Mashiach Ha-Shnia* (Hebrew translation). New York: Fleming H. Revell, 1925.
_____. "Missions." In Needham, *Prophetic Studies of the International Prophetic Conference, 1886.*
_____. "May the United States Intercede for the Jews." *Our Day* 8 (October 1981): 242-43.
_____. "Jerusalem." *The Jewish Era* 1 (1892): 67-71.
_____. "The Jews." *The Jewish Era* 2 (1893): 134-35.
_____. *Satan, His Kingdom and its Overthrow.* Chicago: Fleming H. Revell, 1900.

_____. "Britain Beware." *The Jewish Era* 11 (1902): 46-49.

_____. *The Millennium*. Chicago: Fleming H. Revell, 1904.

_____. *The Heart of the Jewish Problem*. Chicago: Chicago Hebrew Mission, 1905.

_____. *The "Times of the Gentiles" and the Time of the End*. Chicago: Fleming H. Revell, n.d.

_____. "How *Jesus is Coming* Came to be Written." *The Jewish Era* 30 (1921): 171-74.

_____. "Jewish Restoration Past and Present." *The Jewish Era* 32 (1923): 10-12.

Bradford, William. *History of Plymouth Plantation, 1620-1647*. 2 vols. Boston: Massachusetts Historical Society, 1912.

Brookes, James H. *Maranatha: Or the Lord Cometh*. St. Louis: Edward Bredell, 1874.

_____. *"I am Coming" A Setting Forth of the Second Coming of Our Lord Jesus Christ as Personal-Private-Premillennial*. London: Pickering and Inglis, n.d.

_____. "Israel and the Church." *The Truth* 7 (1881): 117-20, 165-69.

_____. "The Purpose of God Concerning Israel as Revealed in the Prophecy by Daniel." *The Truth* 9 (1883): 502-16.

_____. "Jewish Promise." *The Truth* 11 (1885): 211-14.

_____. "How to Reach the Jews." *The Truth* 19 (1893): 134-36.

_____. "To the Jew First." *The Truth* 19 (1893): 325-27.

_____. "Salvation is of the Jews." *The Truth* 19 (1893): 331.

_____. "Work Among the Jews." *The Truth* 20 (1894): 15-16.

_____. *Till He Comes*. Chicago: Fleming H. Revell, 1895.

_____. *Israel and the Church*. Chicago: Fleming H. Revell, n.d.

Burrell, David J. "Signs of the Times." In Gaebelein, *Christ and Glory*.

Cartwright, Peter, *Autobiography of Peter Cartwright*. Nashville: Abingdon Press, 1956.

Darby, John N. *Notes of Sermons*. Dublin: Richard Moore Tims, 1838.

_____. *Letters of John Nelson Darby*. 3 vols. Sudbury, Pennsylvania: Believers Bookshelf, 1971.

Dixon, Amzi C., Louis Meyer, and Reuben A. Torrey, eds. *The Fundamentals: A Testimony to the Truth*. 12 vols. Chicago: Testimony Publishing Co., 1910-1915.

Douglas, Sholto D.C. "The Antichrist: His Character and History." In Erdman, *Addresses of the International Prophetic Conference 1901*.

Erdman, William J. "The Fulness of the Gentiles." In Needham, *Prophetic Studies of the International Prophetic Conference, 1886.*

_____. "The Structure of the Book of Isaiah and Part II. 40-66: A Prediction of Jewish History during the Times of the Gentiles." In Erdman, *Addresses of the International Prophetic Conference 1901.*

_____, ed. *Addresses of the International Prophetic Conference held December 10-15, 1901, in the Clarendon Street Baptist Church, Boston, Mass.* Boston: Watchword and Truth, n.d.

Finley, James B. *Sketches of Western Methodism.* Cincinnati: Methodist Book Concern, 1854.

Freuder, Samuel. *My Return to Judaism.* New York: B. Zuckerman, 1922.

The Fundamentals of the Faith as Expressed in the Articles of Belief of the Niagara Bible Conference. Chicago: Great Commission Prayer League, n.d.

Gaebelein, Arno C. "Herman Warszwiak's Method of Getting Crowds to Hear the Gospel." *Our Hope* 2 (1895): 2-5.

_____. *The Messiah and His People Israel.* New York: Hope of Israel, 1898.

_____. "A Short Review of Our Mission and the Principles of the Hope of Israel Movement." *Our Hope* 6 (1899): 68-71.

_____. *Hath God Cast Away His People?* New York: Gospel Publishing House, 1905.

_____. *The Jewish Question.* New York: Publication Office, "Our Hope," 1912.

_____. *The Work of Christ.* New York: Publication Office, "Our Hope," 1913.

_____. *Current Events in the Light of the Bible.* New York: Publication Office, "Our Hope," 1914.

_____. "The Lord's Coming in Relation to Israel, Symposium." In Gray, *The Coming and Kingdom of Christ.*

_____. "Fulfilled Prophecy, a Potent Argument for the Bible." In Dixon, et al., *The Fundamentals.*

_____. "The Capture of Jerusalem and the Great Future of that City." Gaebelein, *In Christ and Glory.*

_____. "Isaiah Chapter XIX, The Conversion of Egypt." *Our Hope* 27 (1921): 600-606.

_____. "Jewish Leadership in Russia." *Our Hope* 27 (1921): 734-35.

_____. "Aspects of Jewish Power in the United States." *Our Hope* 29 (1922): 103.

_____. "The Same Old Accusation." *Our Hope* 30 (1924): 556.

_____. *Christianity or Religion?* New York: Our Hope, 1927.

_____. *The Christ We Know*. Chicago: Bible Institute Colportage Association, 1927.

_____. "The Middle Wall of Partition." *Our Hope* 34 (1928): 750.

_____. "Adolf Hitler—Will He Be Germany's Dictator?" *Our Hope* 37 (1930): 363-64.

_____. *Half a Century: The Autobiography of a Servant*. New York: Publication Office, "Our Hope," 1930.

_____. "The Shadows of Jacob's Trouble." *Our Hope* 38 (1932): 102.

_____. *The Conflict of the Ages, the Mystery of Lawlessness: Its Origin, Historic Development and Coming Defeat*. New York: Publication Office, "Our Hope," 1933.

_____. *Hopeless—Yet There is Hope*. New York: Publication Office, "Our Hope," 1935.

_____. *The Prophet Daniel*. New York: Publication Office, "Our Hope" 1936.

_____. "Observations and Experiences." *Our Hope* 44 (1938): 461-65, 746-50.

_____. "The Plight of the Austrian Jews." *Our Hope* 44 (1938): 825-26.

_____. "Misrepresenting 'Our Hope.' " *Our Hope* 46 (1939): 379-82.

_____. "Alfred Rosenberg, the German Anti-Christian Leader Speaks Again." *Our Hope* 45 (1939): 688-89.

_____. "The New Great World Crisis: XXIII." *Our Hope* 49 (1943): 813-19.

_____, ed. *Christ and Glory: Addresses Delivered at the New York Prophetic Conference Carnegie Hall, November 25-28, 1918*. New York: Publication Office, "Our Hope," 1919.

Goldberg, Louis. *Turbulence Over the Middle East*. Neptune, New Jersey: Loizeaux Brothers, 1983.

Goodspeed, Edgar J. *A Full History of the Wonderful Career of Moody and Sankey*. Ashland, Ohio: C. C. Wick & Co. Publishers, 1876.

Goodwin, Edwin P. "The Second Coming of the Lord, Personal and Premillennial." In Kyle and Miller, *Addresses on the Second Coming of the Lord*.

Graham, Billy. *World Aflame*. Garden City, New York: Doubleday & Company, 1965.

Gray, James M. *Great Epochs of Sacred History*. New York: Fleming H. Revell, 1910.

_____. "The War and the Jews." *Christian Workers Magazine* 16 (1916): 347-48.

_____. *A Textbook on Prophecy*. New York: Fleming H. Revell, 1918.

_____. "The Capture of Jerusalem." *Christian Workers Magazine* 18 (1918): 447.

_____. "The Jewish Protocols." *Moody Bible Institute Monthly* 22 (1921): 598.

_____, ed. *The Coming and Kingdom of Christ: A Stenographic Report of the Prophetic Bible Conference Held at the Moody Bible Institute of Chicago, February 24-27, 1914*. Chicago: Bible Institute Association, 1914.

Guers, Emile. *Le Destin d'Israel*. Vaud, Suisse: M. Roger Grandchamp, 1964.

Hartzler, H. B. *Moody in Chicago or the World's Fair Gospel Campaign*. New York: Fleming H. Revell, 1894.

Hobart, Chauncey. *Recollections of My Life: Fifty Years of Itinerancy in the Northwest*. Red Wing, Minn.: Red Wing Printing Co., 1885.

Ironside, Henry. *Who will be Saved in the Coming Period of Judgment*. New York: Loizeaux Brothers, n.d.

Kelley, William, ed. *The Collected Writings of J. N. Darby*. 34 vols. Sunbury, Pennsylvania: Believers Bookshelf, 1972.

Kohler, Kaufman. *Jewish Theology*. New York: Macmillan Company, 1918.

_____. *Studies, Addresses and Personal Papers*. New York: Alumni Association of Hebrew Union College, 1931.

_____. *A Living Faith*. Cincinnati: Hebrew Union College Press, 1948.

Kyle, Joseph, and William S. Miller, eds. *Addresses on the Second Coming of the Lord Delivered at the Prophetic Conference, Allegheny, Pa., December 3-6, 1895*. Pittsburgh: W. W. Waters, n.d.

Ladd, George E. *The Blessed Hope*. Grand Rapids, Michigan: Wm. B. Eerdmans Publishing Company, 1960.

Larkin, Clarence. *Dispensational Truth or God's Plan and Purpose in the Ages*. Glenside, Pa.: Published by the author, 1920.

Lesser, A. J. G. *In the Last Days*. Chicago: N. Gonsior, 1897.

Lindsey, Hal. *The Late Great Planet Earth*. Grand Rapids, Michigan: Zondervan Publishing House, 1971.

_____. *The Promise*. Eugene, Oregon: Harvest House Publishers, 1982.

_____. *The Rapture*. New York: Bantam Books, 1983.

Link, Arthur S., ed. *The Papers of Woodrow Wilson.* 45 vols. Princeton, New Jersey: Princeton University Press, 1966-1984.

Mackintosh, C. H. *The Lord's Coming.* Chicago: Moody Press, n.d.

Magoun, George F. "The Chicago Jewish Christian Conference." *Our Day* 7 (1890): 266-71.

Mauro, Philip. *The Hope of Israel—What Is It?* Boston: Hamilton Brothers, 1929.

McCall, Thomas S., and Zola Levitt. *The Coming Russian Invasion of Israel.* Chicago: Moody Press, 1974.

Meeker, Charles. "Evangelization of the American Jew." *Christian Workers Magazine* 19 (1919): 868.

Minutes of the General Assembly of the Presbyterian Church in the United States of America. New series, vol. 16, August 1916. Philadelphia: Office of the General Assembly, 1916.

Moody, Dwight L. *Glad Tidings.* New York: E. B. Treat, 1876.

_____. *To All People.* New York: E. B. Treat, 1877.

_____. *The New Sermons.* New York: H. S. Goodspeed, 1880.

_____. *"To the Work, to the Work!" Exhortations to Christians.* Chicago: Fleming H. Revell, 1880.

_____. *Heaven: Where It Is, Its Inhabitants, and How to Get There.* Chicago: Fleming H. Revell, 1881.

_____. *Twelve Select Sermons.* Chicago: Fleming H. Revell, 1881.

_____. *Great Joy.* New York: E. B. Treat, 1887.

_____. *Overcoming Life and Other Sermons.* New York: Fleming H. Revell, 1896.

_____. "The Second Coming of Christ." In Scofield, *The Second Coming of Christ.*

_____. "The Second Coming of Christ." *Northfield Echoes* 3 (1896): 281.

_____. *The Home Work of D. L. Moody.* New York: Fleming H. Revell, 1896.

_____. *Daily Meditations.* Grand Rapids, Michigan: Baker Book House, 1964.

Moorehead, William G. "The Final Issue of the Age." In Kyle and Miller, *Addresses on the Second Coming of the Lord.*

_____. "The Conversion of the World after the Conversion of the Jews." In Erdman, *Addresses of the International Prophetic Conference 1901.*

Mundhall, Leander W. "The Coming of the Lord and World-Wide Evangelization." In Erdman, *Addresses of the International Prophetic Conference 1901.*

Nason, Elias. *The Lives of the Eminent American Evangelists Dwight Lyman Moody and Ira David Sankey.* Boston: B. B. Russell, 1877.

Needham, George C. "The Future Advent of Jesus." *Northfield Echoes* 1 (1894): 496-99.

_____, ed. *Prophetic Studies of the International Prophetic Conference, Chicago, Ill., November 1886.* Chicago: Fleming H. Revell, 1886.

Nicholson, William R. "The Gathering of Israel." In West, *Second Coming of Christ.*

Owens, J. A. "The Second Advent Era in Bible Perspective." In Kyle and Miller, *Addresses on the Second Coming of the Lord.*

Payne, J. Barton. *The Prophecy Map of World History.* New York: Harper & Row, 1974.

Pettingill, William L. *Israel—Jehovah's Covenant People.* Harrisburg, Pa: Fred Kelker, 1905.

_____. *God's Prophecies for Plain People.* Philadelphia: Philadelphia School of the Bible, 1923.

_____. *Loving His Appearing and Other Prophetic Studies.* Findlay, Ohio: Fundamental Truth Publishers, 1943.

_____. *Nearing the End.* Chicago: Van Kampen Press, 1948.

Pettingill, William L., J. R. Schafler, and J. D. Adams, eds. *Light on Prophecy: A Coordinated, Constructive Teaching being the Proceedings and Addresses at the Philadelphia Prophetic Conference, May 28-30, 1918.* New York: Christian Herald Bible House, 1918.

Philpott, P. W. "Coming Events Cast their Shadow Before." In Pettingill, et al., *Light on Prophecy.*

Rabinowitz, Joseph. *Jesus of Nazareth, The King of the Jews.* Translated from the Jargon, abridged and Revised by Arno C. Gaebelein. New York: Hope of Israel, 1898.

Richards, Le Grand. *Israel! Do You Know?* Salt Lake City: Deseret Book Company, 1954.

Richardson, James D. *A Compilation of the Messages and Papers of the Presidents.* 11 vols. Washington: Government Printing Office, 1817-1898.

Riley, William B. "The Significant Signs of the Times." In Gray, *The Coming and Kingdom of Christ.*

_____. "The Last Times." In Gaebelein, *Christ and Glory.*

_____. *Wanted—A World Leader!* Published by the author, n.d.

Rohold, S. B. *The War and the Jews.* Cincinnati: Standard Publishing Company, 1917.

Scofield, Cyrus I. *Scofield Reference Bible.* New York: Oxford University Press, 1909.

_____. *The Second Coming of Christ.* Chicago: Bible Institute Colportage Association, 1896.

Simons, Laird M. *Holding the Fort Comprising Sermons and Addresses at the Great Revival Meetings Conducted by Moody and Sankey.* Philadelphia: John C. Winston Co., 1880.

Speer, Robert E. *D. L. Moody.* East Northfield, Mass.: Northfield Schools, 1931.

Strack, Hermann L. *Yearbook of the Evangelical Missions Among the Jews.* 2 vols. Leipzig: J.C. Hinrichs'sche Buchhandlung, 1906-1913.

Stroeter, Ernest F. "Christ's Second Coming Premillennial." In Needham, *Prophetic Studies of the International Prophetic Conference, 1886.*

_____. "A Misapprehension Corrected." *Our Hope* 2 (1895): 55-58.

_____. "The Second Coming of Christ in Relation to Israel." In Kyle and Miller, *Addresses on the Second Coming of the Lord.*

Sullins, David. *Recollections of an Old Man: Seventy Years in Dixie, 1827-1897.* Bristol, Tenn.: King Printing Co., 1910.

Thompson, Albert E. *A Century of Jewish Missions.* Chicago: Fleming H. Revell, 1902.

_____. "The Capture of Jerusalem." In Pettingill, et al., *Light on Prophecy.*

Torrey, Reuben A. "Jesus Christ—Notes on Lectures Delivered by R. A. Torrey." *The Institute Tie* 2 (1893): 48-49.

_____. *The Moody Bible Institute Correspondence Department, Bible Doctrines, First Course.* Chicago: Moody Bible Institute, 1901.

_____. *Practical and Perplexing Questions Answered.* Chicago: Fleming H. Revell, 1908.

_____. *The Return of the Lord Jesus.* Los Angeles: Bible Institute of Los Angeles, 1913.

_____. "The Blessed Hope." In Gaebelein, *Christ and Glory.*

Urofsky, Melvin I., and David W. Levy, eds. *Letters of Louis D. Brandeis.* 5 vols. Albany, New York: State University of New York Press, 1971-1978.

Vester, Bertha S. *Our Jerusalem: An American Family in the Holy City, 1881-1949.* Garden City, N.Y.: Doubleday & Company, Inc., 1950.

Van Impe, Jack, and Roger F. Campbell, *Israel's Final Holocaust*. Nashville: Thomas Nelson Publishers, 1979.

Walvoord, John F. *The Rapture Question*. Findlay, Ohio: Dunham Publishing Co., 1957.

_____. *Israel in Prophecy*. Grand Rapids, Michigan: Zondervan Publishing House, 1962.

West, Nathaniel. "History of the Premillennial Doctrine." In West, *Second Coming of Christ*.

_____. "Prophecy and Israel." In Needham, *Prophetic Studies of the International Prophetic Conference, 1886*.

_____, ed. *Second Coming of Christ, Premillennial Essays of the Prophetic Conference Held in the Church of the Holy Trinity, New York City*. Chicago: Fleming H. Revell, 1879.

Wilkinson, Samuel. "The Moral Defensibility of some of the Methods Employed in Jewish Missions." In Strack, *Yearbook of the Evangelical Missions among the Jews*.

Wise, Stephen P. *Challenging Years*. New York: G. P. Putnam's Sons, 1949.

SECONDARY SOURCES

Adler, Cyrus, and Aaron M. Margalith, *With Firmness in the Right: American Diplomatic Action Affecting Jews, 1840-1945*. New York: American Jewish Committee, 1946.

Adler, Selig. "The Palestine Question in the Wilson Era." *Jewish Social Studies* 10 (1948): 303-34.

Ahlstrom, Sydney E. *A Religious History of the American People*. Vols. 1-2. Garden City, New York: Image Books, 1975.

Albanese, Catherine L. *America Religions and Religion*. Belmont, California: Wadsworth Publishing Company, 1981.

Arrington, Leonard J., and Davis Bitton. *The Mormon Experience*. New York: Alfred A. Knopf, 1979.

Barr, James. *Fundamentalism*. Philadelphia: Westminster Press, 1978.

_____. *The Scope and Authority of the Bible*. Philadelphia: Westminster Press, 1980.

Bass, Clarence B. *Background to Dispensationalism*. Grand Rapids, Michigan: Eerdmans Publishing Company, 1960.

Beegle, Davey M. *Prophecy and Prediction*. Ann Arbor, Michigan: Pryor Pettengill, 1978.

Brodeur, David D. "Christians in the Zionist Camp: Blackstone and Hechler." *Faith and Thought* 100 (1972-3): 271-98; 101 (1974): 44-70.

Case, Shirley J. *The Millennial Hope*. Chicago: University of Chicago Press, 1918.

Coad, Roy F. *A History of the Brethren Movement*. Exeter: Paternoster Press, 1968.

Cohen, Naomi W. *Encounter with Emancipation: The German Jews in the United States 1830-1914*. Philadelphia: Jewish Publication Society, 1984.

Cohn, Norman. *Warrant for Genocide: The Myth of the Jewish World-Conspiracy and the Protocols of the Elders of Zion*. London: Eyre & Spottiswoode, 1967.

Cox, William E. *An Examination of Dispensationalism*. Philadelphia: Presbyterian and Reformed Publishing Co., 1963.

Curtis, Richard K. *They Called Him Mister Moody*. Garden City, N.Y.: Doubleday, 1962.

Davis, Moshe, ed. *With Eyes Toward Zion, Scholars Colloquium on America—Holy Land Studies*. New York: Arno Press, 1977.

_____, ed. *Christian Protagonists for Jewish Restoration*. New York: Arno Press, 1977.

_____. *Holy Land Missions and Missionaries*. New York: Arno Press, 1977.

Ehle, Carl F., Jr. "Prolegomena to Christian Zionism in America: The Views of Increase Mather and William E. Blackstone Concerning the Doctrine of the Restoration of Israel." Ph.D. dissertation, New York University, 1977.

Ehlert, Arnold D. *A Bibliographic History of Dispensationalism*. Grand Rapids, Michigan: Baker Book House, 1965.

Eichhorn, David M. *Evangelizing the American Jew*. Middle Village, N.Y.: Jonathan David Publishers Inc., 1978.

Encyclopaedia Judaica. S.v. "Christian Zionism," by Yona Malachy.

Encyclopedia of Zionism and Israel. S.v. "Restoration Movement," by Yona Malachy.

Epstein, Lawrence J. *Zion's Call, Christian Contributions to the Origins and Development of Israel*. Lanham, Md.: University Press of America, 1984.

Feinstein, Marnin. *American Zionism, 1884-1904*. New York: Herzl Press, 1965.

Festinger, Leon. *When Prophecy Fails*. Minneapolis: University of Minnesota Press, 1956.

Findlay, James F. *Dwight L. Moody: American Evangelist 1837-1899*. Chicago: University of Chicago Press, 1969.

Fink, Reuben. *America and Palestine*. New York: Herald Square Press, 1945.

Flusser, David. "The Reflection of Jewish Messianic Beliefs in Early Christianity." In *Messianism and Eschatology*. Edited by Zvi Baras [in Hebrew]. Jerusalem: Zalman Shazar Center, 1983.

Friedman, Isaiah. *The Question of Palestine, 1914-1918, British—Jewish—Arab Relations*. London: Routledge & Kegan Paul, 1973.

Froom, Le Roy E. *The Prophetic Faith of Our Fathers*. 4 vols. Washington, D.C.: Review and Herald, 1946-1954.

Gaebelein, Frank E. *The Story of the Scofield Reference Bible*. New York: Oxford University Press, 1959.

Garret, Clarke. *Respectable Folly*. Baltimore: Johns Hopkins University Press, 1975.

Gavish, Dov. "The American Colony and its Photographers." In *Zev Vilnay's Jubilee Volume*. Edited by Ely Schiler [in Hebrew]. Jerusalem: Ariel Publishing House, 1984.

Glazer, Nathan. *American Judaism*. Chicago: University of Chicago Press, 1972.

Glock, Charles Y., and Rodney Stark. *Christian Beliefs and Anti-Semitism*. New York: Harper & Row, 1966.

Grabill, Joseph L. *Protestant Diplomacy and the Near East: Missionary Influence on American Policy, 1810-1927*. Minneapolis: University of Minnesota Press, 1971.

Grose, Peter. *Israel in the Mind of America*. New York: Alfred A. Knopf, 1983.

Gundry, Stanley N. *Love Them In, The Proclamation Theology of D. L. Moody*. Chicago: Moody Press, 1976.

Haddad, Hassan, and Donald Wagner, eds., *All in the Name of the Bible*. Chicago: PHRC Special Report # 5, 1985.

Halpern, Ben. *A Clash of Heroes*. New York: Oxford University Press, 1987.

Halsell, Grace. *Prophecy and Politics: Militant Evangelicals on the Road to Nuclear War*. Westport, Connecticut: Lawrence Hill & Company, 1986.

Handy, Robert T. "Zion in American Christian Movements." In *Israel: Its Role in Civilization*. Edited by Moshe Davis. New York: Jewish Theological Seminary, 1956.

_____. *A Christian America: Protestant Hopes and Historical Realities.* New York: Oxford University Press, 1981.

_____, ed. *The Holy Land in American Protestant Life, 1800-1948.* New York: Arno Press, 1981.

Harrison, J. F. C. *The Second Coming, Popular Millenarianism 1780-1850.* New Brunswick: Rutgers University Press, 1979.

Holmes, Reed M. *The Forerunners.* Independence, Mo.: Herald Publishing House, 1981.

Katz, David S. *Philo-Semitism and the Readmission of the Jews to England, 1603-1655.* Oxford: Clarendon Press, 1982.

Keck, Sandy. "W. E. Blackstone, Champion of Zion" (a series of 11 articles). In *American Messianic Fellowship Monthly* 78-79 (1973-74).

Klausner, Israel. "Adam Rosenberg: One of the Earliest American Zionists." *Herzl Year Book* 1 (1958): 232-87.

Kobler, Franz. *The Vision was There.* London: Lincolns-Prager, 1956.

Kraus, C. Norman. *Dispensationalism in America.* Richmond, Virginia: John Knox Press, 1958.

Latourette, Kenneth Scott. *A History of the Expansion of Christianity.* Vol. 4. New York: Harper and Brothers, 1941.

Libman-Lebeson, Anita. "Zionism Comes to Chicago." In Meyer, *Early History of Zionism in America.*

Lindberg, Beth M. *A God-Filled Life: The Story of William E. Blackstone.* Chicago: American Messianic Fellowship, n.d.

Littell, Franklin H. *The German Phoenix.* New York: Doubleday, 1960.

MacPherson, Dave. *The Incredible Cover Up: The True Story of the Pre-Tribulation Rapture.* Omega Publications: Plainfield, N.J., 1975.

_____. *The Great Rapture Hoax.* Fletcher, North Carolina: New Puritan Library, 1983.

Madsen, Truman G. *The Mormon Attitude Toward Zionism.* Haifa: The University of Haifa, 1982.

Malachy, Yona. *American Fundamentalism and Israel.* Jerusalem: The Institute of Contemporary Jewry, Hebrew University of Jerusalem, 1978.

Manuel, Frank E. *The Realities of American-Palestine Relations.* Washington, D.C.: Public Affairs Press, 1949.

Marsden, George M. *Fundamentalism and American Culture: The Shaping of Twentieth-Century Evangelicalism, 1870-1925.* New York: Oxford University Press, 1982.

Marty, Martin E. *Righteous Empire.* New York: Dial Press, 1970.

_____. *A Nation of Behavers*. Chicago: University of Chicago Press, 1976.

_____. *Pilgrims in Their Own Land: 500 Years of American Religion*. Boston: Little, Brown and Company, 1984.

_____. *Modern American Religion Vol. 1: The Irony of it All, 1893-1919*. Chicago: University of Chicago Press, 1986.

McLoughlin, William G. *Modern Revivalism: Charles Grandison Finney to Billy Graham*. New York: Ronald Press Company, 1959.

_____. *Revivals, Awakenings, and Reform*. Chicago: University of Chicago Press, 1978.

Meyer, Isidore S, ed. *Early History of Zionism in America*. New York: American Jewish Historical Society and Theodor Herzl Foundation, 1958.

Miller, Perry, and Thomas H. Johnston. *The Puritans*. New York: American Book Company, 1938.

Mouly, Ruth W. *The Religious Right and Israel: The Politics of Armageddon*. Chicago: Midwest Research, 1985.

Murray, Iain H. *The Puritan Hope*. London: Banner of Truth Trust, 1971.

Niebuhr, H. Richard. *The Kingdom of God in America*. New York: Harper, 1937.

Naor, Mordecai. "The Settlement of the Americans in Jaffa." In *Zev Vilnay's Jubilee Volume*. Edited by Ely Schiler [in Hebrew]. Jerusalem: Ariel Publishing House, 1984.

Oliver, W. H. *Prophets and Millennialists*. Auckland, New Zealand: Auckland University Press, 1978.

Polish, David. *Renew Our Days, The Zionist Issue in Reform Judaism*. Jerusalem: World Zionist Organization, 1976.

Pragai, Michael J. *Faith and Fulfillment, Christians and the Return to the Promised Land*. London: Valentine, Mitchell and Company, 1985.

Rausch, David A. *Zionism Within Early American Fundamentalism, 1878-1918*. New York: Edwin Mellen Press, 1978.

_____. "Arno C. Gaebelein (1861-1945): Fundamentalist Protestant Zionist." *American Jewish History* 68 (1978): 43-56.

_____. "Our Hope: An American Fundamentalist Journal and the Holocaust, 1937-1945." *Fides et Historia* 12 (1980): 89-103.

_____. "Fundamentalism and the Jew: An Interpretive Essay." *Journal of the Evangelical Theological Society* 23 (1980): 102-12.

_____. "A Rejoinder to Timothy Weber's Reply." *Journal of the Evangelical Theological Society* 24 (1981): 73-77.

_____. *Messianic Judaism: Its History, Theology, and Polity*. New York: Edwin Mellen Press, 1982.

_____. *Arno C. Gaebelein, 1861-1945: Irenic Fundamentalist and Scholar*. New York: Edwin Mellen Press, 1983.

Ribuffo, Leo P. "Henry Ford and the International Jew." *American Jewish History* 69 (1980): 437-77.

Ricks, Eldin. "Zionism and the Mormon Church." *Herzl Year Book*. Vol. 5. Edited by Raphael Patai. New York: Herzl Press, 1963.

Rooy, Sidney H. *The Theology of Missions in the Puritan Tradition*. Delft: W.D. Meinema, 1965.

Roy, Ralph L. *Apostles of Discord*. Boston: Beacon Press, 1953.

Ryrie, Charles C. *Dispensationalism Today*. Chicago: Moody Press, 1965.

Safran, Nadav. *Israel the Embattled Ally*. Cambridge, Massachusetts: Belknap Press of Harvard University Press, 1981.

Sandeen, Ernest R. *The Roots of Fundamentalism*. Grand Rapids, Michigan: Baker Book House, 1978.

Scult, Mel. *Millennial Expectations and Jewish Liberties*. Leiden: E. J. Brill, 1978.

Sharif, Regina S. *Non-Jewish Zionism, Its Roots in Western History*. London: Zed Press, 1983.

Smith, Wilbur M. *An Annotated Bibliography of D. L. Moody*. Chicago: Moody Press, 1948.

Sobel, B. Z. *Hebrew Christianity: The Thirteenth Tribe*. New York: John Wiley & Sons, 1974.

Stein, Leonard. *The Balfour Declaration*. London: Valentine, Mitchell and Co., 1961.

Toon, Peter, ed. *Puritans, the Millennium and the Future of Israel*. London: James Clarke & Co., 1970.

Tuchman, Barbara W. *Bible and Sword*. London: Macmillan, 1983.

Tuveson, Ernest L. *Redeemer Nation, The Idea of American Millennial Role*. Chicago: University of Chicago Press, 1968.

Urofsky, Melvin I. *American Zionism from Herzl to the Holocaust*. Garden City, N.Y.: Anchor Press/Doubleday, 1975.

Weber, Timothy P. "A Reply to David Rausch's 'Fundamentalism and the Jew.' " *Journal of the Evangelical Theological Society* 24 (1981): 67-71.

_____. "A Surrejoinder to David Rausch's Rejoinder." *Journal of the Evangelical Theological Society* 24 (1981): 79-82.

_____. *Living in the Shadow of the Second Coming: American Premillennialism 1875-1982*. Grand Rapids, Michigan: Zondervan Publishing House, 1983.

Whitwell, Cutler B. "The Life Story of William E. Blackstone and of 'Jesus is Coming.' " *The Sunday School Times*, 11 January 1936: 19-20. Repr. *The Jewish Era* 46 (1936): 64-67.

Wilson, Dwight. *Armageddon Now! The Premillennarian Response to Russia and Israel Since 1917*. Grand Rapids, Michigan: Baker Book House, 1977.

Index

Chicago Studies in the History of American Religion

Editors

JERALD C. BRAUER & MARTIN E. MARTY

(continued, over)